THE FORMS OF POETRY

The FORMS OF POETRY

A Pocket Dictionary of Verse

By Louis Untermeyer

REVISED EDITION

HARCOURT, BRACE & COMPANY
New York   1942

POETRY

DEFINED BY SIX POETS

The poet's eye, in a fine frenzy rolling,
Doth glance from heaven to earth, from earth to heaven;
And as imagination bodies forth
The forms of things unknown, the poet's pen
Turns them to shapes, and gives to airy nothings
A local habitation and a name.
—*William Shakespeare*

Poetry is the imaginative expression of strong feeling, usually rhythmical . . . the spontaneous overflow of powerful feelings recollected in tranquility.—*William Wordsworth*

The proper and immediate object of Science is the acquirement or communication of truth; the proper and immediate object of Poetry is the communication of pleasure . . . I wish our clever young poets would remember my homely definitions of prose and poetry; that is, *prose:* words in their best order; *poetry:* the best words in the best order.
—*Samuel Taylor Coleridge*

If I read a book and it makes my whole body so cold no fire can ever warm me, I know that is poetry. If I feel physically as if the top of my head were taken off, I know that is poetry. These are the only ways I know it. Is there any other way?—*Emily Dickinson*

Poetry is a language that tells us, through a more or less emotional reaction, something that cannot be said. All poetry, great or small, does this. And it seems to me that poetry has two outstanding characteristics. One is that it is, after all, undefinable. The other is that it is eventually unmistakable.—*Edwin Arlington Robinson*

It is absurd to think that the only way to tell if a poem is lasting is to wait and see if it lasts. The right reader of a good poem can tell the moment it strikes him that he has taken an immortal wound—that he will never get over it. That is to say, permanence in poetry as in love is perceived instantly. It hasn't to await the test of time. The proof of a poem is not that we have never forgotten it, but that we knew at sight we never could forget it.—*Robert Frost*

FOREWORD

The purpose of this book is explained by its subtitle: it is a pocket dictionary of verse, not an encyclopedic survey. It has been prepared in response to the requests of many teachers and students for a concise handbook. It is in no sense an erudite or exhaustive analysis for scholars. It pretends to be nothing more than a simple compendium for beginners and readers interested in the craft of poetry. It is, in short, a volume for the novice, not a profound examination like Lascelles Abercrombie's *The Theory of Poetry*. The definitions, though at times necessarily technical, are as brief as possible without sacrificing any important point; the quotations are meant to serve as illustrations, not only to " beautify " the text, but to heighten an appreciation of the forms themselves.

When this volume was first conceived, it was intended as a companion volume to *Yesterday and Today: A Comparative Anthology of Poetry*, but its scope is such that it can be used with any collection of poems. It is, however, particularly applicable to the study of modern poetry (by which term is meant the poetry of the last hundred years) and the various patterns—fixed and free —which it employs.

Detailed acknowledgments cannot possibly be made in this instance. Reference has been made to a wide variety of sources, all of which have been noted in " A Summarized Bibliography." The sestina (" The Conqueror Passes ") by James Branch Cabell has been reprinted from his volume of verse, *From the Hidden Way*, by permission of the author and the publishers,

Robert M. McBride and Company. The "Villanelle, with Stevenson's Assistance" is quoted from *Weights and Measures* by Franklin P. Adams by permission of the publishers, Doubleday, Page and Company, who have also given their consent to the use of a paragraph from *Creative Youth* by Hughes Mearns. It might be added that special aid has been given by a study of Gleeson White's *Ballades and Rondeaus, Sestinas, Etc.*, and by the suggestions of Winifred Howell Davies, who is also responsible for the plan as well as a great part of the chapter, "A Brief Outline of English Poetry."

It remains to say that the deeper purpose of these pages is the winning of the reader's interest in the structure as well as the spirit of poetry. Love of any art is increased by knowledge of its forms, its grammar, its laws of composition and harmony. To him who understands counterpoint, a symphony is something more than a progression of beautiful sounds; it is a miracle of "molten architecture." It is hoped that this volume not only will foster a fuller appreciation of the sonnet, the ballade, and the very framework of verse, but—if the metaphysical metaphor is not too extravagant—will reveal the glories of the body not less than the soul of poetry.

May, 1926

L. U.

CONTENTS

THE FORMS OF POETRY

A HANDBOOK OF POETIC TERMS
(The arrangement is alphabetical.)

Alexandrine. Alexandrine verse, the most popular measure in French poetry, originated in the thirteenth century. It was composed of lines twelve syllables in length (hexameter), and, until the rigidity of the form came to be ignored by modern poets, was strictly regulated as to pauses. Two laws were recognized: (1) each line should have two equal parts, the sixth syllable always ending a word and not being merely an isolated syllable; (2) there should be no " run-on " lines—that is, no overlapping from one line to the next.

Although the Alexandrine remains the regular line of the French heroic couplet, it has never found much favor among the English poets. Michael Drayton was the first to employ it in England (*c.* 1590). An Alexandrine, as we know it today, is an iambic line of twelve syllables, or thirteen if the rhyme is doubled or " feminine," but always of six accents. Its employment at the end of shorter-line stanzas gives an effect of dignity. Spenser discovered this and used it consistently; in the Spenserian stanza it becomes the last (and longest) line of each verse. Pope, who found it heavily pompous, characterized it when he wrote:

A needless Alexandrine ends the song,
That, like a wounded snake, drags its slow length along.

Alliteration. Alliteration is the repetition of the same sound, in words succeeding each other at close intervals. Usually it refers to the repetition of a sound or letter at the beginning of words, like:

Fields ever fresh and groves ever green.

But, besides the repetition of the *f* and *g* in this line, there is alliteration in the *v* sounds, half buried in the midst of the words. A famous example, is the use of *m* sounds in these lines of Tennyson's:

3

> The moan of doves in immemorial elms,
> And murmur of innumerable bees.

Little Nathalia Crane, at the age of ten, unconsciously follows Swinburne in her love of this musical effect. She speaks of " pansies painted in postures," and she sees how

> Conquered by confusing quests,
> The doves drift down to dine.

Swinburne allowed his love for alliteration to run riot, the following couplet being famous for its excesses:

> The lilies and languors of virtue
> And the raptures and roses of vice.

Swinburne has been parodied so often that many readers see nothing in this poet but the wearying repetition of his consonants; the creator himself burlesqued his weakness in one of the cleverest parodies ever written. " Nephelidia " is not only a brilliant piece of nonsense but a remarkable piece of self-criticism. These are the first two lines:

> From the depth of the dreamy decline of the dawn through
>   a notable nimbus of nebulous noonshine,
> Pallid and pink as the palm of the flag-flower that
>   flickers with fear of the flies as they float.

Antistrophe. (See **Strophe,** page 34.)

Assonance. Assonance means the *resemblance* rather than the correspondence of sound—the latter being *rhyme*. Rhyme is an exact matching of the vowel sound; assonance is an approximation of it. *Earth* and *birth,* *late* and *fate, willow* and *pillow* are rhymes; *earth* and *hearth, late* and *fade, willow* and *yellow* are assonances.

Amy Lowell and John Gould Fletcher make a particularly lavish use of assonance as an additional ornamentation; Walter de la Mare is fond of pairing such words as *grass* and *was, moon* and *gone;* John Crowe Ransom, among others, has been experimenting in such "off-color" or "oblique" or "suspended" rhymes as *little* and *beetle*, *lady* and *study*, *fallen* and *sullen*, while Humbert Wolfe, one of the most delightful of recent lyricists, achieves charming effects by playing almost exclusively on such assonances and half-rhymes as *false* and *else*, *trouble* and *pebble*, *Paris* and *cherries*. (In lieu of quotation, the student is referred to John Gould Fletcher's *Breakers and Granite*, Amy Lowell's *Can Grande's Castle* and *Legends*, John Crowe Ransom's *Chills and Fever*, Humbert Wolfe's *The Unknown Goddess*, and *A Miscellany of American Poetry—1925* for many instances of the recent popularity of assonance.)

Ballad. (Listed under "The Forms of Poetry" on page 39.)

Ballade. (Listed under "The Forms of Poetry" on page 43.)

Ballade à Double Refrain. (Listed under "The Forms of Poetry" on page 48.)

Blank Verse. (Listed under "The Forms of Poetry" on page 50.)

Bucolic Poetry. (See **Pastoral Poetry,** page 29.)

Burden. (See **Refrain,** page 31.)

Caesura. A caesura (also spelled *cesura*) is a pause in a line or at the end of a line of verse, a slight break made to accentuate the beat of the rhythm. It often divides the line into more or less equal parts. The following is an example of the use of the caesura at the end of the second foot:

> Man never is, ‖ but always to be blessed.
> —*Pope*

The following is an even more distinct use of the break within one line:

> The gods are dead? ‖ Perhaps they are! ‖ Who knows?
> —*Henley*

Cadence. Cadence, originally a musical term, signifies the close of a musical passage or phrase. In its more general sense, it denotes a fall of the voice in reading or speaking, as at the end of a sentence. Applied to modern poetry, its meaning is similar. The late Amy Lowell said that free verse should really be called *cadenced* verse, "as it is built upon 'organic rhythm,' or the rhythm of the speaking voice with its necessity for breathing." (For fuller details, see **Free Verse**.)

Chant Royal. (Listed under "The Forms of Poetry" on page 52.)

Cinquain. (Considered as **Quintet** under "The Forms of Poetry" on page 68.)

Classical. In general, the word *classical* in literature and the fine arts denotes a purity of outline as well as a refinement of feeling. It is usually used in opposition to *romantic* or *realistic*. In modern literature, *classical* rarely refers to the great creators of ancient Greece or Rome, but to the appreciation which is aroused by the actual *form* of a work of art. The critic, Roger Fry, has expressed the difference between *romantic* and *classical* in these sentences:

> I call romantic any work of art which to produce its effect counts on the *association of ideas* which it sets up in the mind of the spectator. I call classical the work which to provoke emotion depends on its own *formal* organization.

Cliché. The word *cliché*, which the modern poets have brought into use, is originally a French word, meaning an electrotype, or a die used many hundreds of times for the same impression. Applied to poetry, a cliché is a word or phrase which has been used over and over until it becomes so stereotyped, so overfamiliar, that it no longer has any effect of surprise upon the reader.

Thus the phrases *rosy dawn, boundless blue, break of day, fall of night,* originally conveyed striking images; to-day, they are clichés, or as we might say in English rubber-stamp expressions which have been repeated so often and have grown so commonplace that the reader is scarcely aware of their poetic significance. Some of the other outworn poeticisms are: *silvery moon, caressing winds, stately lilies, red as a rose, old as the hills, pure as snow, smooth as silk, hair like spun gold, modest violet, playful breezes.* These and dozens of other hackneyed expressions are seldom used by representative poets and the young writer does well to avoid them.

One of the best examples of the cliché in the classroom —and the students' reaction to it—is given in a passage in *Creative Youth,* a volume which illustrates, by method and example, the way literature is made to live in the Lincoln School in New York City. I quote the following fragment (and the delicious double parody) from the chapter by Hughes Mearns, entitled "Method in Certain Cases."

A lively-witted girl began to write rapidly, and with studied ostentation. In a moment she broke into the general talk with "Is *fluffy cloud* a *cliché?*" The laugh that followed answered her. She appeared dramatically dejected, gazing open-eyed at her paper as if she had just surprised a bug there. "But not *boundless blue?*" The laugh was even more tempestuous. "And *molten gold?* and *dewy earth?*" The class confirmed her worst fears, to speak pure *cliché.* "But surely," she brightened up, "*fettered soul* is—" Her sentence was lost in a shout. She shook her head, murmuring, "*Rosy sunset,* of course; and *hazy blue;* yes, I see," and dropped her manuscript with a delightful affectation of despair. "Someone is always taking the poetry out of life," she said.

Immediately she cheered up and began again with mock zeal to write; this time she was flying to catch up with the very wind of inspiration. Shortly I received the following illustration of the effectiveness of our teaching, a thing I treasure as a triumph of personal pedagogy:

B. C. (Before Cliché)

Morning

I watched a fluffy cloud drift by
Across the boundless blue of sky
And saw the sun's rays, molten gold,
Upon the dewy earth unfold.

Evening

I felt my fettered soul uplift
Before the rosy sunset drift
And in the hazy blue afar
I saw the gleaming evening star.

A. D. (After Discovering—'em)

Morning

I saw the sun with battered face
Trying to warm the human race;
I watched a sodden cloud limp by
Like some discouraged custard pie.

Evening

The sleepy sun in flannels red
Went yawning to its Western bed;
I saw one shivering small star
No brighter than our dishpans are.
—*Jewell Martin*

Conceit. In the literary sense, a conceit is a witty conception or ingenious thought; a diverting or highly fanciful idea. A brief piece of imaginative writing which is neither too flippant nor too profound is often referred to as "a happy *conceit.*" The Elizabethans were particularly fond of these playfully conceived inventions; Donne and the writers of his time brought them to a point where they often became monstrous and sometimes absurd. Thomas Campion was one who came perilously close to the limits of prettiness, particularly in the following set of conceits:

> There is a Garden in her face,
> Where roses and white Lilies grow;
> A heav'nly paradise is that place,
> Wherein all pleasant fruits do flow.
> There Cherries grow which none may buy
> Till Cherry ripe themselves do cry.
>
> Her Eyes like Angels watch them still;
> Her Brows like bended bows do stand,
> Threat'ning with piercing frowns to kill
> All that attempt, with eye or hand,
> Those sacred Cherries to come nigh,
> Till Cherry ripe themselves do cry.
> —*Thomas Campion*

Richard Crashaw, in an effort to achieve a striking metaphor, reaches the very height of the ridiculous in his conceit describing the Magdalene's eyes as

> Two welling baths, two weeping motions,
> Portable and compendious oceans.
> —*Crashaw*

Couplet. (Listed under "The Forms of Poetry" on page 55.)

Dactyl. (See *fourth* subdivision under **Foot,** page 16.)

Dactylic Hexameter. (See **Blank Verse** under "The Forms of Poetry.")

Dimeter. Dimeter is a line of verse which has only

two feet or measures. Hood's "Bridge of Sighs" depends almost entirely on dimeter for its effect, as, for example:

Take her up || tenderly,
Lift her with || care;
Fashioned so || slenderly,
Young and so || fair.

Distich. (The same as **Couplet,** listed under "The Forms of Poetry" on page 55.)

Elegy. An elegy means exactly what the Greek word *elegos* originally meant: a lament, a song of mourning. An elegy may be a poem on the death of a person or a composition expressing a more general sorrow. Among the famous elegies in English verse, the four greatest are Milton's "Lycidas," Shelley's "Adonais," Gray's "Elegy in a Country Churchyard," and Whitman's "When Lilacs Last in the Dooryard Bloom'd."

Envoy. The envoy is the concluding half-stanza which ends every ballade. (For a detailed description of the ballade, see "The Forms of Poetry.") It is also used in a more general sense, as a postcript to a composition or an epilogue to a work.

Epic. Possibly the outstanding characteristic of the epic is the immensity of its theme. It sums up the entire spirit of an age and, in its heroic sweep, transcends that age. Further than this, it embodies the conflict of two great forces, as in the struggle between good and evil in Milton's *Paradise Lost* and Dante's *Divine Comedy*. The epic often revolves about the exploits of some national hero: Homer's *Iliad* and *Odyssey* center about Odysseus and the wars of Greece and Troy; Vergil's *Aeneid* celebrates Aeneas; *The Song of the Nibelungs* tells the tale of Siegfried; *The Song of Roland* is an idealization of the Gallic spirit. An American epic is still to be made of the mythical hero of the lumber-camps, the Herculean Paul Bunyan and the legend of Johnny Appleseed.

Epigram. An epigram in verse is a short poem which is confined to one subject and usually finishes with an ingenious turn of thought. Sometimes it is merely a pointed saying happily expressed in rhyme; often, however, it holds a large idea condensed in a packed space. Excellent examples of epigrams may be found in practically every anthology, especially in the section entitled "The Barb of Satire" in *The Home Book of Verse*. There is no rule as to length; the greatest number of epigrams, however, seem to be in quatrains, although some of the very finest epigrams have been written in two lines (couplets).

Coleridge's definition is, in itself, one of the best that has ever been attempted:

> What is an Epigram? A dwarfish whole;
> Its body brevity, and wit its soul.

The Eighteenth Century, with its love of pointed wit and barbed elegance, was particularly hospitable to the epigram. There was scarcely a poet of this period who did not take advantage of these brief and brilliant thrusts; some of the keenest epigrams in the language have been written by poets as polished as Pope and as mystical as Blake. Three of the most famous (surprising in their modernity) are the following:

> You beat your pate, and fancy wit will come.
> Knock as you please,—there's nobody at home.
> > —*Alexander Pope*

> This house, where once a lawyer dwelt,
> > Is now a smith's. Alas!
> How rapidly the iron age
> > Succeeds the age of brass!
> > > —*William Erskine*

> Great things are done where men and mountains meet;
> These are not done by jostling in the street.
>
> —*William Blake*

An even shorter example is the proverb attributed to Benjamin Franklin:

> Little strokes
> Fell great oaks.

Epitaph. An epitaph, in the common use of the word, is an inscription on a monument in memory of the dead. In poetry, it is a verse either composed for the occasion or merely used for the purpose of honoring the deceased. Certain epitaphs have a strong epigrammatic and even satirical flavor. Two of the most famous are the following:

> Life is a jest, and all things show it;
> I said so once, and now I know it.
>
> —*John Gay*

> Here lie I, Martin Elginbrodde:
> Hae mercy o' my soul, Lord God,
> As I wad do were I Lord God
> And ye were Martin Elginbrodde.
>
> —*George Macdonald*

Among modern poets, none has written more vivid and clenched epitaphs than the little known Englishwoman, Sylvia Townsend Warner. Her volume, *The Espalier*, has several brilliant examples—all quatrains—from which the following two are reprinted:

> After long thirty years re-met
> I, William Clarke, and I, Jeanette
> His wife, lie side by side once more;
> But quieter than we lay before.

❖

> John Bird, a laborer, lies here,
> Who served the earth for sixty year

With spade and mattock, drill and plough;
But never found it kind till now.
                    —*Sylvia Townsend Warner*

Epithet. An epithet is an adjective which expresses some striking or especially revealing quality of the thing to which it is applied. The difference between "a yellow topaz" and "a sun-bright topaz" is the difference between a mere adjective and an epithet.

Euphuism. Euphuism is an ornate elegance and over-refinement of speech. The term is taken from Euphues, an affected character in John Lyly's work of that name. It is often used to denote the avoidance of a simple phrase by the substitution of a piece of high-flown diction. When a certain writer, refusing to call a spade a spade, refers to it as "a sharpened tongue of iron, hungry for the earth," he is employing a Euphuism. This use of odd comparisons and lavish constructions influenced many of Lyly's contemporaries. Neilson and Thorndike (in their *History of English Literature*) maintain that "in spite of its affectations, its main influence was good, for it helped to teach English prose the advantages of balance and firmness of structure."

Figure. A figure of speech has been said to be " the essential stuff of poetry." The very element of poetry is surprise. Wonder is most effectually achieved by an unexpected suggestion or association of some familiar object with one remote or hitherto unassociated. The two most common figures are *metaphor* and *simile*.

A Metaphor is that figure of speech which is *directly* founded on the resemblance one object bears to another—a comparison which is made or, rather, implied without any preposition ("as" or "like") to express the comparison. When Emily Dickinson speaks of a snake whiplash unbraiding in the sun" or calls frost "the assassin" she is employing a metaphor.

A Simile is a metaphor which employs the word "as" or "like" to express the comparison. When Burns wrote "O, my luve's like a red, red rose" he was using a simile; had he written "O, my luve *is* a red, red rose" he would have used a metaphor. "He is a stubborn ox" is a metaphor; "he is as stubborn *as* an ox" is a simile.

(*Metonymy* and *Synecdoche* are other and less common figures of speech, defined in alphabetical order.)

Fixed Forms. (Listed under "The Forms of Poetry" on page 56.)

Foot. A foot (or measure) is a certain number of syllables constituting part of a line of verse; each syllable corresponds to a beat in a bar of music. In charting the various kinds of feet, the authorities have devised a way of measuring them by dividing the syllables into long, or accented, beats (designated by the symbol —) and short, or unaccented, beats (designated by the symbol ⌣).

It should be understood that practically no poem is composed *entirely* of iambic, dactylic, anapestic, or trochaic measures. Verse built on any one foot or stress would become monotonous and tiresome. Moreover, it is almost impossible to construct a poem without employing a variety of feet. Almost all poets use combinations of the various measures—the measure of a line being determined from the foot which happens to *predominate*.

According to the pedagogues, there are about thirty combinations of long and short syllables, most of them being found in Greek and Latin versification. However, the five most common in English verse are called as follows:

1. The Iambus (or Iamb), a short syllable followed by a long one, is expressed thus: ‿ —. Words like *afraid, oppose, correct, delight* are, in themselves, an iambic foot. The iambus is the most common foot of all; it might almost be said that English verse is founded upon it. There are so many examples of it in this volume that it is impossible to list them. The greater part of Shakespeare, practically all of the ballads, and most of the folksongs are based on the iambic measure. One of the most beautiful as well as one of the most perfect examples of the iambic line is the exquisite lyric of Robert Burns which begins:

> Ŏ, mȳ | lŭve's līke | ă rĕd, | rĕd rōse
> That's newly sprung in June:
> O, my luve's like the melodie
> That's sweetly played in tune.

2. The Trochee, a long syllable followed by a short one, is expressed thus: — ‿. A complete trochaic foot is found in words like *gather, going, heartless, laughter*. This foot is only a trifle less common than the iambus. Its light and happy nature has been particularly attractive to the singers; lyric poetry is full of it. The strongly stressed (accented) first syllable can be discovered on almost every page of this collection. Among the older examples, this stanza from "A Cradle Hymn" by Isaac Watts is an excellent illustration:

> Sōft ănd | ēasȳ | īs thȳ | crādlĕ:
> Coarse and hard thy Saviour lay,
> When His birthplace was a stable
> And His softest bed was hay.

3. The Spondee, two long syllables following each other, is expressed thus: — —. This is rarely used, as there are few instances in which it can serve as anything more than a substitute foot. One finds it in poetry as a variation of the rhythm. Some words which, in themselves, are perfect spondees are: *heartbreak, childhood, bright-eyed, bookcase, wineglass, Mayday*—most of them being combinations of two nouns.

4. *The Dactyl,* a long syllable followed by two short ones, is expressed thus: — ˘ ˘. Three-syllable words accented on the first syllable, like *happiness, drearily, satisfy, merriment, century,* represent a dactylic foot. The dactyl and the anapest often slide into each other, as no line of verse can maintain so decided a beat without variation. It is not used nearly as often as the first two feet, but it is particularly effective in certain poems where speed, a lilting movement, or even a gallop is desired. A perfect example of the dactyl is Tennyson's:

Love again, | song again, | nest again, | young again.

5. *The Anapest,* two short syllables followed by one long one, is expressed thus: ˘ ˘ —. Three-syllable words accented on the last syllable constitute an anapest. For example: *interrupt, Viennese, supersede, disappear.* A well known illustration of the anapest is afforded by the line:

With the sheep | in the fold | and the cows | in their stalls.

There are two other feet which are sometimes, though rarely, found in English poetry, and they are the Amphibrach and the Amphimacer.

6. *The Amphibrach,* a trio of short, long, and short syllables, is expressed thus: ˘ — ˘

7. *The Amphimacer,* a trio of long, short, and long syllables, is expressed thus: — ˘ —

Metrical Feet

Trochee trips from long to short.
From long to long in solemn sort
Slow Spondee stalks; strong foot! yet ill able
Ever to come up with Dactyl trisyllable.
Iambics march from short to long;—
With a leap and a bound the swift Anapests throng.
One syllable long, with one short at each side,
Amphibrachys haste with a stately stride;—
First and last being long, middle short, Amphimacer
Strikes his thundering hoofs like a proud high-bred Racer.
                              —*Samuel Taylor Coleridge*

Free Verse. Free verse, or, as it is sometimes called by its French equivalent, *vers libre*, is based upon a broad (and often irregular) movement rather than on a fixed pattern; it might be said to be founded on a *general* rhythm rather than on any precise meter. The late Amy Lowell, a pioneer as well as one of the greatest modern exponents of this form, said that "since verse is verse just *because* it has more pattern than prose, free verse is a misnomer; verse can never be free. The best name for this form in English would be 'cadenced verse' for it is based upon cadence rather than upon actual meter. Metrical verse seeks its effects chiefly through definite lilt of meter and the magic and satisfaction of chime. 'Cadenced verse' gets its effects through subtle shades of changing rhythms and through a delicate sense of balance."

The unit of free verse is the *strophe*, not the line or the foot as in regular meter. The strophe, in Greek drama, was the full circle made by the chorus while walking about the altar, chanting the ode. The length of time varied, but it was always one completed movement. Therefore, the strophe applied to modern verse means

one completed round (a cadence), or a series of such
units. In short free-verse poems the strophe may be the
entire poem; in longer ones there is usually a succession
of strophes. However, though free verse dispenses with
any decided meter, it employs all the other assets of
poetry: assonance, alliteration, balance—even, though
not always, rhyme. In fact, it differs from formal
poetry only in its irregularity of rhythm. It is actually
not so different from other verse when we hear it; it
merely *looks* stranger. And this should not confuse the
reader. A poem, after all, must make its chief appeal
to the ear and not to the eye. And, no matter how the
poet may choose to divide his lines, it is the rise and fall
of his speech that we listen to—if our ears remain open.

Although there has been a great interest in free verse
recently, it is by no means a new departure. In America,
Walt Whitman blazed a path for all followers as early
as 1860, when his tremendous *Leaves of Grass* startled
two continents. In England, Henley's *Echoes* and *London
Voluntaries* contained many instances of this flexible form,
and Heinrich Heine, possibly greatest of lyric poets, gave
full expression not only to this form but to the ocean itself
in his two sweeping cycles entitled *The North Sea*. But
an even older precedent is the Bible. It was, as we all
know, originally written in Hebrew poetry. But how
many are aware of the fact that Hebrew poetry is a kind
of "cadenced verse"? Hebrew poetry is actually built
on balance: instead of rhyme, it uses similar consonants
(alliteration); instead of a set meter, it employs the
"strophic" measure. The King James Version recaptures
much of the ancient music. When we read the Psalms,
the Song of Solomon, and the Book of Job, we are reading
the greatest free verse that has ever been written. If
printed according to its natural cadences, a few of the

lines from God's tremendous questions to Job would
appear thus:

> Hast thou given the horse strength?
> Hast thou clothed his neck with thunder?
> Canst thou make him afraid as a grasshopper?
> The glory of his nostrils is terrible.
> He paweth in the valley, and rejoiceth in his strength;
> He goeth on to meet the armed men.
> He mocketh at fear, and is not affrighted,
> Neither turneth he back from the sword.
> The quiver rattleth against him,
> The glittering spear and the shield,
> He swalloweth the ground with fierceness and rage;
> Neither believeth he that it is the sound of the trumpet.
> He saith among the trumpets, Ha, ha!
> And he smelleth the battle afar off.
>
> . . . .
>
> Where wast thou when I laid the foundations of the earth?
> Declare, if thou hast understanding.
> Who hath laid the measures thereof, if thou knowest,
> Or who hath stretched the line upon it?
> Whereupon are the foundations thereof fastened?
> Or who laid the cornerstone thereof,
> When the morning stars sang together,
> And all the sons of God shouted for joy?

French Forms. The French Forms or, as they are
sometimes called, *Fixed Forms* are as old as the Fourteenth Century and, as the name indicates, are of French
origin. They enjoyed their greatest favor in France
from the beginning of the Fifteenth to the end of the
Seventeenth Century. The middle of the Nineteenth
Century witnessed a revival of interest in these precise
and highly artificial modes, and this renewed interest
made them popular both in England and America. A
more detailed account of these forms as well as an explanation of their chief divisions (the Ballade, the Rondeau,

the Rondel, the Triolet, etc.) will be found under "The Forms of Poetry."

Hexameter. Hexameter is a line of verse which has six metrical feet. The *Iliad* of Homer and the *Aeneid* of Vergil are examples of classical hexameter. Longfellow's *Evangeline* is almost entirely composed in this measure:

This is the | forest pri|meval.   The | murmuring | pines and the | hemlocks,
Bearded with moss, and in garments green, indistinct in the twilight.

Hyperbole. Hyperbole, in spite of its forbidding appearance, is a word which means nothing more nor less than exaggeration. Hyperbole is used by all of us continually to add force or intensity to a statement. Shakespeare is particularly fond of its use—he achieves an effect of genuine horror when he has Lady Macbeth cry, "All the perfumes of Arabia will not sweeten this little hand."

Sometimes, however, the use of exaggeration can reach the very limits of the ridiculous. The famous instance of absurd hyperbole is the limerick:

> There was a young lady of Lynn
> Who was so uncommonly thin
>   That when she essayed
>   To drink lemonade,
> She slipped through the straw and fell in.

Iambus. (See first subdivision under **Foot,** page 15.)
Iambic Pentameter. (Listed under "The Forms of Poetry" as **Blank Verse** on page 50.)
Idyl. An idyl (also spelled idyll) is a poem, usually short, representing simple objects in nature or scenes of pastoral life. (See **Pastoral Poetry.**) The most famous of the ancient poems of this type are the Idyls of

Theocritus; the best known modern example is Tennyson's *Idylls of the King*.

Interior Rhyme. Interior rhyme, or, as it is often called, *internal rhyme*, is merely the repetition of the rhyme-sound *within* the line or inside the structure of the poem itself. An example of three internal rhymes within a single line is Wallace Irwin's "Song for a Cracked Voice," which begins:

> When I was young and slender, a spender, a lender,
>   What gentleman adventurer was prankier than I,
> Who lustier at passes with glasses—and lasses,
>   How pleasant was the look of 'em as I came jaunting by!

Sometimes the interior rhyme is found at the beginning instead of at the end of a line. An example of this is Thomas Hood's "The Double Knock," which starts out:

> "Rat-tat" it went upon the lion's chain;
> "That hat, I know it!" cried the joyful girl;
> "Summer's it is, I know him by his knock;
> Comers like him are welcome as the day!
> Lizzy! go down and open the street-door;
> Busy I am to any one but him.
> Know him you must—he has been often here;
> Show him upstairs, and tell him I'm alone."

Kipling is very fond of the device of internal rhyming. His poem "Tomlinson" ends:

> That the sin they do by two and two they must pay for one by
>   one—
> And the god that you took from a printed book be with you,
>   Tomlinson!

Two of the more complicated examples of interior rhyming—in which the rhymes occur not only at the ends but in the middle and beginnings of the lines, making curious and surprising patterns of their own—

are "Boy and Tadpoles" (in *Yesterday and Today*) and
"Roast Leviathan," the title poem of the editor's own
volume. A fragment of the latter is quoted, with the
interior rhymes in italics:

> It is the final Day.
> A *blast* of *Gabriel's horn* has *torn* away
> The *last haze* from our *eyes*, and *we* can *see*
> *Past* the *three* hundred *skies* and *gaze* upon
> The Ineffable Name engraved deep in the *sun*.
> Now *one* by one, the *pious* and the just
> Are seated *by us*, radiantly *risen*
> From their dull *prison* in the dust. . .
> And then the festival *begins!*
> A sudden music *spins* great webs of *sound*
> Spanning the *ground*, the stars and their *companions;*
> While from the cliffs and *cañons* of blue *air*,
> *Prayers* of *bold* colors, *cries* of exultation
> *Rise* into *choruses* of singing gold.
> And at the *height* of this *bright* consecration,
> The whole *Creation's rolled before us*.

Inversion. Inversion is a change in the natural order
of words. It was formerly used in an effort to emphasize
certain words by placing them in a position where
ordinarily they would not be found. It is almost unused
to-day by the better poets, being indulged in only by
versifiers who have difficulty with their rhythm. For
example, the sentence: "A moonlit mist fills the valley,
though the moon, herself, rides unseen," in the hands of a
poor craftsman becomes such an awkward piece of versification as:

> A moonlit mist the valley fills,
> Though rides unseen herself the moon.

One of the objects of modern poetry is a straight-
forwardness, a directness of speech, and hence inversion

is frowned upon. It may be added that in *vers de société*, where the verse is supposed to be the clever talk of clever people, inversion is not merely inappropriate but is absolutely forbidden.

Kenning. Kenning is a device employed in Anglo-Saxon poetry (from the Seventh to the Eleventh Century) and is a curious archaic figure of speech, practically unknown now, though widely used in the early days. In *A History of English Literature*, by Neilson and Thorndike, it is defined as follows: "A kenning is a kind of metaphor, in which the simple name of anything is replaced by a phrase describing one of its functions or qualities; thus, 'ring-giver' is used for king, 'hearth-companions' for his attendant warriors, 'swan's bath' or 'whale's road' for sea, 'sea-wood' for ship. These occur in great numbers."

Light Verse. (See **Vers de Société**.)

Lyric. A lyric (from the Greek word *lyrikos*) was originally a song sung to the accompaniment of the lyre. In an age that has dispensed with lyres, the term means nothing more definite than "a song." A lyric has no particular length or structure; its one requirement is that it must *sing*.

> I would be the Lyric
> Ever on the lip,
> Rather than the Epic
> Memory lets slip.
> —*Thomas Bailey Aldrich*

Measure. (See **Foot**.)

Metaphor. (See **Figure**.)

Meter. This term is taken from a Greek word meaning *measure*. In verse it means a regular succession of beats arranged according to some particular pattern. It is distinguished from rhythm by the fact that *rhythm* is the measure of time by strophe or stress rather than by definite beat. Meter, in short, is a decidedly *regular* accent, whereas rhythm is variable.

Metonymy. Metonymy is a figure of speech which, though not nearly so common as metaphor and simile, is often employed by the poets. *Metonymy* and *synecdoche* are so like each other that the terms are often confused and it has become the custom to use metonymy for both. *Metonymy* is that figure in which a part is used for the whole in order to make the entire picture more effective by focusing the attention upon one detail. Strictly speaking, metonymy is a substitution of one word for another—as we say "We enjoy Keats" when we mean that we enjoy the writings of Keats, or "Set the table" when we mean to set the dishes on the table, or "The kettle is boiling" when we mean that the water in the kettle is boiling.

Synecdoche is actually that figure in which the detail is used to suggest the entire thing. Thus when Kipling refers to England holding "Dominion over palm and pine," he suggests, by the selection of the typically northern and southern trees, the extent of the Empire over which England rules.

Monometer. Monometer is a line of verse made of only one metrical foot, and is introduced, as a rule, to give variety to the pattern of the poem. Although one rarely finds entire poems which are constructed wholly of lines which have a single beat, a few examples exist. One of the best is Herrick's "Upon His Departure Hence."

> Thus I
> Passe by,
> And die:
> As One,
> Unknown,
> And gone.

I'm made
A shade,
And laid
I' th' grave:
There have
My Cave.
Where tell
I dwell,
Farewell.

(The rhymes of this poem, by the way, are built on a set of tercets, or triplets.)

Narrative Verse. As the name indicates, narrative verse is that kind of poetry which tells a story. A narrative poem has no particular form, and, although it may contain lyrical or descriptive passages, its chief object is to relate a particular event or to tell a long tale.

Naturalistic. (See **Realistic.**)

Occasional Poetry. The phrase "occasional poetry" has two meanings. In one sense it means what the term implies: a poem written for an occasion. Poems celebrating a birthday, a marriage, the founding of an institution are, generally speaking, occasional poems. Most elegies also come under this head. In its other sense, occasional poetry is another term for *vers de société*.

Octave. (Listed under "The Forms of Poetry" on page 60.)

Ode. (Listed under "The Forms of Poetry" on page 62.)

Onomatopoeia. Onomatopoeia is the formation of a word by imitating some particular sound; the syllables thus formed suggest the object which produces the sound. It is the simplest and oldest form of speech; many specialists believe that all language had its origin in this principle. Babies learn to recognize things by associating them with the sound they produce: they employ onomatopoeia naturally by naming the sound—bow-wow is a dog, ding-dong is a bell, buzz-buzz is a fly, choo-choo is a locomotive, moo-moo is a cow. The poet relies almost as much on this method: *hum, whiz, crash, twitter, whir, crackle, slush, swish, jangle, crunch* are all onomatopoetic words. Even a reader with little or no knowledge of Latin can hear the gallop of a horse in the beat of the words:

> Quadrupedente putrem sonitu quatit ungula campum.

Among the living American poets, Vachel Lindsay has been particularly happy in the use of these sound-words. His "Kallyope Yell" is an attempt to put the whole spirit of howling democracy into the tone of the street calliope.

> Music of the mob am I,
> Circus day's tremendous cry:—
> I am the Kallyope, Kallyope, Kallyope!
> Tooting hope, tooting hope, tooting hope;
> Hoot toot, hoot toot, hoot toot, hoot toot,
> Willy willy willy wah Hoo!
> Sizz, fizz. . . . [1]

Ottava Rima. (Considered under "The Forms of Poetry" on page 61.)

Parody. In a broad sense, parody is an imitation of a particular style so exaggerated or distorted as to be humorous. When it is merely a ridiculous twisting of an author's words or some slight alteration of his phrases, it is *burlesque*. Possibly the most quoted example of this type is Catherine Fanshawe's burlesque of Alexander Pope's lines. Pope's famous couplet runs:

> Here shall the Spring its earliest sweets bestow!
> Here the first roses of the year shall blow!

[1] From *Collected Poems* by Vachel Lindsay. The Macmillan Company, publishers. Copyright, 1923.

By a change of one word and one letter, Catherine Fanshawe achieves this ludicrous result:

> Here shall the Spring its earliest colds bestow!
> Here the first noses of the year shall blow!

True parody is not only a humorous mimicry of some author's manner but also a critical interpretation of his style.

Some of the best known authors may be numbered among the world's most notable parodists. A. C. Swinburne, Bayard Taylor, William Makepeace Thackeray, Phoebe Cary, Lewis Carroll, Bret Harte, the brothers Horace and James Smith, and Charles S. Calverley are possibly the most famous parodists of the past. Among contemporary writers who have brought this "critical diversion" to a remarkably high plane are Anthony C. Deane, J. C. Squire, Owen Seaman, F. S. (the modest signature of Frank Sidgwick, parodist and publisher), Max Beerbohm, J. K. Stephens, and, though his parodies are practically unknown, Rudyard Kipling. Taylor was particularly successful in his parodies of the classics; Deane is more adroit in lampooning his confrères. The neatest of these is Deane's treatment of the theme of "Jack and Jill" as it might have been enlarged into a ballad by Rudyard Kipling (see *Yesterday and Today*) and his use of another nursery rhyme as a strict ballade by Andrew Lang, as follows:

> Unhappy is Bo-Peep,
>   Her tears profusely flow,
> Because her precious sheep
>   Have wandered to and fro,
>   Have chosen far to go,
> For "pastures new" inclined,
>   (See "Lycidas")—and lo!
> Their tails are still behind!

How catch them while asleep?
   (I think Gaboriau
For machinations deep
   Beats Conan Doyle and Co.)
   But none a hint bestow
Save this, on how to find
   The flocks she misses so—
"Their tails are still behind!"

This simple faith to keep
   Will mitigate her woe,
She is not Joan, to leap
   To arms against the foe
   Or conjugate τύπτω;
Nay, peacefully resigned
   She waits, till time shall show
Their tails are still behind!

Bo-Peep, rejoice! Although
   Your sheep appear unkind,
Rejoice at last to know
   Their tails are still behind!
              —*Anthony C. Deane*

The editor, in his *Including Horace*, has presumed to show how the Horatian ode which begins "Integer vitae" might have been paraphrased by some thirty poets, ancient and modern, rewriting the original thought in their own idiom. The following parody is an attempt to show the sort of rondeau that Austin Dobson might have constructed upon the classic lines:

An upright man need never dread
The blows of Fate; he who has led
   A blameless life is safer far
   Than kings in frowning castles are,
For he is armed with Truth instead.

Once, as I roamed with careless tread,
A wolf who heard me turned and fled.

He felt that I was, more than czar,
An upright man.

So when the last refrain is said
Above my narrow, rose-strewn bed,
    Say not, "He worshiped flower and star."
    Say not, "He loved *sans* let or bar."
But write these words above my head:
    "An Upright Man."
                                    —*Louis Untermeyer*

Pastoral Poetry. A pastoral poem is one which describes the life and customs of shepherds or those who dwell close to the soil. The bucolics of Vergil are the most famous examples in older literature. Since the days of the Elizabethans, English poetry has been full of the pastoral note, from the nature poetry of Wordsworth to the almost chirping lyrics of W. H. Davies. In America, the greatest living pastoral poet is undoubtedly Robert Frost, whose bucolics of New England are sure of a lasting place— *North of Boston*, *Mountain Interval*, and *New Hampshire* constituting a triple landmark in our literature.

Pentameter. Pentameter is a line of verse which has five metrical feet. It is almost as common as tetrameter; it is the norm of blank verse, practically all of Shakespeare's dramas being written in this measure:

How far that little candle throws his beams!
So shines a good deed in a naughty world.
                                    —*William Shakespeare*

Pindaric Ode. (Listed under "The Forms of Poetry" on page 64.)

Polyphonic Prose. Polyphonic prose is a cross between poetry and prose. It is a form originated by the French poet. Paul Fort, and employed by the American poets John Gould Fletcher and Amy Lowell. On the printed page it appears as prose, but to the ear it has a definite though irregular poetic structure. "Polyphonic" means "many-voiced," and the form is so called because, according to Miss Lowell, "it makes use of all the 'voices' of poetry, viz.: meter, *vers libre*, assonance, alliteration, rhyme, and balance. It employs every form of rhythm, even prose rhythm at times, but usually holds no particular one for long."

John Gould Fletcher's "Clipper-Ships" is an example of this form. The very opening lines are rich in all the varied effects of this new "orchestral" combination of prose and poetry. (To call attention to the way in which the rhyme and assonance are interwoven, I have taken the liberty of printing some of the syllables in italics.)

Beautiful as a tiered *cloud*, skysails set and *shrouds* twanging, she *emerges* from the *surges* that keep running *away* be*fore day* on the *low* Pacific *shore*. With the *roar* of the wind *blow*ing *half* a *gale after*, she heels and lunges, and buries her bows in the smother, *lift*ing them *swift*ly, and scattering the glistening *spray*-drops from her jib-*sails* with *laughter*.[1]

An equally vivid example is Amy Lowell's fantastic war picture, "The Bombardment," which may be found on page 228 of her *Men, Women, and Ghosts*, besides being quoted in various anthologies.

Prosody. Prosody is that part of grammar which treats of accent and of the ways of versification.

Quatrain. (Listed under "The Forms of Poetry" on page 64.)

Quintet. (Listed under "The Forms of Poetry" on page 68.)

---

[1] From *Breakers and Granite* by John Gould Fletcher. Reprinted by permission of the publishers, The Macmillan Company. Copyright, 1921.

Realistic. The *realistic* or *naturalistic* method is not merely the use of actual things as subjects, but the manner of writing about them in a natural way, in an undecorated, direct expression. As opposed to the *classical* or *romantic* artists, the realists describe nature or life *exactly* as it appears to them. The realist is not concerned with making the world brighter or better; he leaves that to the romanticist. He is satisfied with telling the truth, the whole truth, and—unfortunately too often—nothing but the truth.

Refrain. A refrain (in former times called a *burden*), generally speaking, is nothing more than a chorus—a phrase or a few lines repeated at the end of different stanzas. This is its general meaning. Applied to the ballade, it has a different significance and refers specifically to the *last line* of each stanza.

Rhyme (sometimes spelled *rime*). The matter of what actually constitutes rhyme has been in dispute for a long time. The English language is not nearly so rich in rhyme as most other tongues, and therefore so many liberties have been taken by the poets that it is hard to draw the line between a "perfect rhyme" and a false one. The Elizabethans were fond of pairing such words as *love* and *prove*, *heaven* and *even*, *together* and *wither*— combinations which the purists would say are only "sight-rhymes" and therefore not rhymes at all. However, there are definite laws for rhymes—even though most of the poets have delighted in breaking the rules. In "The Rhymester," Tom Hood (son of the famous poet, Thomas Hood) laid down the following principles: "A rhyme must commence on an accented syllable. From the accented vowel of the syllable to the end, the two or more words intended to rhyme must be *identical* in sound—but the letter or letters preceding the accented vowel must be *unlike* in sound." Thus *night, unite, knight* are not rhymes at all, for even though the spelling is different, there is nothing unlike in the *sound* of the letter preceding the vowel. Thus also *slay* and *sleigh* cannot be said to rhyme, as they have exactly the same sound. In order to rhyme, there must be a *contrast* of sound immediately before the same-sounding accented vowel. This is as true of single rhymes (*night, write, height, kite*, etc.) as in double rhymes (*daughter, water, slaughter*, etc.) or triple rhymes (*rarity, charity, clarity*, etc.). There are many variations of rhyme itself and other effects which are closely related to it. For further reference, see **Interior Rhyme, Alliteration,** and **Assonance.**

Rhythm. Rhythm, in general, is the measure of a movement (not necessarily a single line) by more or less regular recurring accents. It is an arrangement of words with a certain balance and underlying emphasis, an emphasis, however, which is not so regular that it can be reduced to a law. When it *is* reduced to a law, it becomes the *measured* rhythm known as *meter*. Classic poetry has both meter and rhythm; the poetry of Walt Whitman and the Psalms have rhythm without meter.

Rhythm is the base of poetry because it is also a fundamental principle of life. Before man groped to intelligence he must have been influenced by the rhythm of the tides, the regular progression of day and night, the ordered march of the seasons, the very breathing of his body. The babe is rocked with an even motion, sung to and swung in rhythmic measures. "The child," as Robert Lynd has pointed out, "is a poet from the age at which he learns to beat a silver spoon on the table. He likes to make not only a noise, but a noise with something of the regularity of an echo. Later on, he himself trots gloriously in reins with bells that jingle in rhythm as he runs. His pleasure in swings, in sitting behind a horse, in traveling in a train, with its puff as regular as an uncle's watch and its wheels thudding out endless hexameters on the lines, arise from the same delight in rhythm. We may even trace the origins of the poet in those first reduplications of sound that lead a child to call a train a *puff-puff* and its mother *ma-ma*. Cynics may pretend that it is nurses and foolish parents who invent the language of babyhood. It is the child, however, who feels that sound does not mean enough till it has rhymed itself double, and who of its own accord will gravely murmur 'cawr-cawr' to a scratching hen or 'wow-wow' to a dog with expectant eyes and ears."

If this is true—and what scientists can arise to dispute it?—it is little wonder that the entire race has "lisped in numbers," since rhythm is not only in the very elements which surround man, but stirs within him with every throb of his pulse.

Rime Royal. (Listed under "The Forms of Poetry" as **Septet** on page 77.)

Rispetto. (Listed under "The Forms of Poetry" on page 69.)

Romantic. In general, the word *romantic*, applied to art or literature, denotes a highly imaginative quality. It is usually used in opposition to *classical* or *realistic*. The romantic writer pays little attention to the accepted traditions or forms (like the classical writer) and little to the actualities (like the realist); he places more stress on fancy and emotion.

Rondeau. (Listed under "The Forms of Poetry" on page 70.)

Rondeau Redoublé. (Listed under "The Forms of Poetry" on page 74.)

Rondel. (Listed under "The Forms of Poetry" on page 75.)

Roundel. (Listed under "The Forms of Poetry" on page 76.)

Rune. A rune, in general, is a dark or mysterious saying; the word seems to have sprung up among the Scandinavian tribes and originally meant a secret. In poetry, a rune has a special significance applied to early Anglo-Saxon literature. Here it took on something of the character of an anagram and an allegory combined.

Septet. (Listed under "The Forms of Poetry" on page 77.)

Sestet. (Listed under "The Forms of Poetry" on page 78.)

Sestina. (Listed under "The Forms of Poetry" on page 79.)

Simile. (See **Figure**.)

Sonnet. (Listed under "The Forms of Poetry" on page 82.)

Spondee. (See third subdivision under **Foot**, page 15.)

Stanza. A stanza (commonly called a *verse*) is a number of lines of a regular pattern. A poem is a unit made up of a succession of stanzas.

Strophe. The strophe, which originated at the time of classic Greek drama, was the imaginary circle made by the chorus about the center of the stage, as the singers went from right to left, the antistrophe being the reverse. Its use in connection with modern poetry is explained in detail under **Free Verse**.

Synecdoche. (See **Metonymy**.)

Tercet. (Listed under "The Forms of Poetry" as **Triplet** on page 93.)

Tetrameter. Tetrameter is a line of verse which has

four metrical feet. This is one of the commonest meters used, most lyrics being formed on this extremely simple pattern.

> Maid of Athens, ere we part,
> Give, oh, give me back my heart!
> Or, since that has left my breast,
> Keep it now, and take the rest!
> —*Lord Byron*

Trimeter. Trimeter is a line of verse which has three metrical feet.

For example, Herrick's:

> And teach me how to sing
> Unto the lyric string
> My measure ravishing.

Triolet. (Listed under "The Forms of Poetry" on page 92.)

Triplet. (Listed under "The Forms of Poetry" on page 93.)

Trochee. (See second subdivision under **Foot**, page 15.)

Vers de Société. Although there have been many attempts to find an English equivalent for *vers de société*, no English phrase has ever proved a successful substitute for the French term. *Light verse* comes nearest to it, although various editors have suggested *society verse*, *familiar verse*, *occasional verse*. Locker-Lampson called his own collection *Lyra Elegantiarium*, but, although elegance is one of the requirements of *vers de société*, one would scarcely translate this into English as *Elegant Verse!* Carolyn Wells, an assiduous compiler of the lighter forms, has suggested *gentle verse*, saying that "gentle verse would imply lines written of the gentlefolk, for the gentlefolk, and by the gentlefolk."

Although the actual translation of the phrase remains in dispute, there is no disagreement concerning the intrinsic quality of *vers de société*. Its chief characteristics are polish, *savoir-faire*, an ease of expression and, first and last, lightness of touch. Locker-Lampson, in his preface, which is a model of its kind, says: "Occasional Verse should be short, graceful, refined, and fanciful, not seldom distinguished by chastened sentiment, and often playful. The tone should not be pitched high; it should be terse and idiomatic, and rather in the conversational key. The rhythm should be crisp and sparkling, the rhyme frequent and never forced, while the entire poem should be marked by tasteful moderation, high finish and completeness. For, however trivial the subject matter may be, subordination to the rules of composition and perfection of execution is of the utmost importance."

Innumerable examples may be found in the various anthologies devoted to this form, from Locker-Lampson's early collections to *The Little Book of Society Verse* (compiled by Fuess and Stearns). Locker-Lampson's own poems constitute some of the best examples of *vers de société* ever written, and though a dozen other examples might be chosen from the works of Praed, Landor, Prior, and Moore, no neater set of rhymes could be offered than the following:

My Mistress's Boots

They nearly strike me dumb,—
I tremble when they come
    Pit-a-pat:
This palpitation means
These Boots are Geraldine's—
    Think of that!

O, where did hunter win
So delicate a skin
  For her feet?
You lucky little kid,
You perish'd, so you did,
  For my Sweet.

The faëry stitching gleams
On the sides, and in the seams,
  And reveals
That the Pixies were the wags
Who tipt these funny tags,
  And these heels.

What soles to charm an elf!
Had Crusoe, sick of self,
  Chanced to view
One printed near the tide,
O, how hard he would have tried
  For the two!

For Gerry's debonair,
And innocent and fair
  As a rose;
She's an Angel in a frock,—
She's an Angel with a clock
  To her hose!

The simpletons who squeeze
Their pretty toes to please
  Mandarins,
Would positively flinch
From venturing to pinch
  Geraldine's!

Cinderella's *left* and *rights*
To Geraldine's were frights:
  And I trow
The Damsel, deftly shod,
Has dutifully trod
  Until now.

Come, Gerry, since it suits
Such a pretty Puss (in Boots)
    These to don,
Set your dainty hand awhile
On my shoulder, Dear, and I'll
    Put them on.
           —*Locker-Lampson*

Vers Libre. (See **Free Verse,** page 17.)

Verse. In general, verse is that division of literature which is opposed to prose. Although it is often difficult to determine the difference between what we call "verse" and "poetry," it may be said that the difference is one of degree, of literary attitude: the lower forms are light verse, *vers de société*, parody, etc.; in its higher aspect, verse becomes poetry.

In a more specific sense, a verse is the short division of any composition into its parts. When we speak of a verse of poetry, we may refer either to one stanza or to a single line.

Villanelle. (Listed under "The Forms of Poetry" on page 93.)

THE FORMS OF POETRY

Ballad. The ballad (not to be confused with the ballade) in a general sense is a narrative poem (usually short) which is either adapted for singing or, by the use of a refrain, gives the effect of a song. A ballad is thus a combination of narrative and lyrical poetry. There are two distinct types: the popular ballad, which is usually anonymous, and the literary ballad, whose authorship we can trace to a definite poet.

There is a great difference of opinion regarding the origin of the popular ballad. Some authorities believe that it started like the folk-song, as something chanted for a dance accompaniment. Others dispute the theory that the ballad "just grew," like a poetic Topsy; they believe that each ballad was composed by a definite minstrel and, being repeated by others so often before the days of printing, assumed many changes from the original. "A legend," Amy Lowell once wrote, "is something which nobody has written, and everybody has written, and which anybody is at liberty to rewrite." This is equally true of popular ballads, which are, first and last, poetry of the people.

The subjects of the ballads are many. Often they are heroic deeds, or feuds, or grim murders, or tragedies of love. Sometimes an entire cycle revolves about the life of some Homeric outlaw, like the series of ballads about Robin Hood. Quiller-Couch divides his excellent *Oxford Book of Ballads* into seven parts. The first section deals with magic and the supernatural; the second (and the most beautiful) with stories of sheer romance; the

39

third with romance shading off into real history; the fourth
with carols and ballads of Holy Writ; the fifth with the
greenwood and the adventures of Robin Hood; the sixth
follows history from Chevy Chase to the less renowned
Border warfare; the seventh presents the decline of the
ballad into artifice.

After the days of the Scottish ballads, the popular
ballads suffered, since the isolated people who used to
sing them came into contact with civilization and ex-
changed their rude but genuine poetry for cheap and
sentimental melodies. In modern times, however, many
of the poets have recreated this form. No one has ever
captured the spirit of balladry better than Walter Scott.
In the "Rime of the Ancient Mariner," Coleridge has
embodied its ghostly essence. Among the living English
poets, Rudyard Kipling and Alfred Noyes have assumed
prominence as ballad writers. In America, the pioneers
and trail-makers produced many ballads which are as
stirring as they are native. The Kentucky mountain
songs, founded on imported versions, differ from the
English originals so greatly that they have a quality all
their own. The Negroes, bringing to America their
gift of song, have added several high notes to our
literature. And the western cowboys have not only
adapted old ballads to their own use, but composed
many swinging story-poems of the log fire and the cattle
trail.

Among the finest as well as the most famous of ancient
ballads are "Thomas the Rhymer," "Binnorie," "Sir
Patrick Spens," "Clerk Saunders," "Childe Waters,"
"Young Hunting," "Fair Margaret and Sweet William,"
"Edward, Edward," and "Lord Randal." The last has
many variations, of which the best though possibly the
least known is

Lord Donald

" O where hae ye been a' day, Lord Donald, my son?
O where hae ye been a' day, my jolly young man? "
" I've been awa courtin':—mither, mak my bed sune,
For I'm sick at the heart, and I fain would lie doun."

" What wad ye hae for your supper, Lord Donald, my son?
What wad ye hae for your supper, my jolly young man? "
" I've gotten my supper:—mither, mak my bed sune,
For I'm sick at the heart, and I fain would lie doun."

" What gat ye for your supper, Lord Donald, my son?
What gat ye for your supper, my jolly young man? "
" A dish of sma' fishes;—mither, mak my bed sune,
For I'm sick at the heart, and I fain wad lie doun."

" O I fear ye are poison'd, Lord Donald, my son!
O I fear ye are poison'd, my jolly young man! "
" O yes! I am poison'd:—mither, mak my bed sune,
For I'm sick at the heart, and I fain wad lie doun."

" What will ye leave to your father, Lord Donald, my son?
What will ye leave to your father, my jolly young man? "
" Baith my houses and land:—mither, mak my bed sune,
For I'm sick at the heart, and I fain wad lie doun."

" What will ye leave to your brither, Lord Donald, my son?
What will ye leave to your brither, my jolly young man? "
" My horse and the saddle:—mither, mak my bed sune,
For I'm sick at the heart, and I fain wad lie doun."

" What will ye leave to your sister, Lord Donald, my son?
What will ye leave to your sister, my jolly young man? "
" Baith my gold box and rings:—mither, mak my bed sune,
For I'm sick at the heart, and I fain wad lie doun."

" What will ye leave to your true-love, Lord Donald, my son?
What will ye leave to your true-love, my jolly young man? "
" The tow and the halter, for to hang on yon tree,
And lat her hang there for the poisoning o' me."

Modern poets, as has already been implied, have enriched literature with many ballads which, though not so direct and "folk-like" as the old, have the fundamental qualities of this form. A small anthology of recent ballads might be selected from the works of Rudyard Kipling, Alfred Noyes, G. K. Chesterton, John Masefield—to say nothing of those immortal burlesques, *The Bab Ballads* by W. S. Gilbert—and from the more local examples of Longfellow, Amy Lowell, and the brothers in balladry, William Rose Benét and Stephen Vincent Benét. Space curtails quotation, but as an example of a modern ballad which retains the true folksong flavor, this little-known poem by W. E. Henley (who informs us that the chorus is old) is worthy of the reader's study:

Home

O, Falmouth is a fine town with ships in the bay,
And I wish from my heart it's there I was today;
I wish from my heart I was far away from here,
Sitting in my parlor and talking to my dear.
    For it's home, dearie, home—it's home I want to be.
Our topsails are hoisted, and we'll away to sea,
O, the oak and the ash and the bonnie birken tree
They're all growing green in the old countrie.

In Baltimore a-walking a lady I did meet
With her babe on her arm, as she came down the street;
And I thought how I sailed, and the cradle standing ready
For the pretty little babe that has never seen its daddie.
    And it's home, dearie, home—it's home I want to be.
Our topsails are hoisted, and we'll away to sea.
O, the oak and the ash and the bonnie birken tree
They're all growing green in the old countrie.

O, if it be a lass, she shall wear a golden ring;
And if it be a lad, he shall fight for his king;

With his dirk and his hat and his little jacket blue,
He shall walk the quarter-deck as his daddie used to do.
    And it's home, dearie, home—it's home I want to be.
    Our topsails are hoisted, and we'll away to sea.
    O, the oak and the ash and the bonnie birken tree
    They're all growing green in the old countrie.

O, there's a wind a-blowing, a-blowing from the west,
And that of all the winds is the one I like the best,
For it blows at our backs, and it shakes our pennon free,
And it soon will blow us home to the old countrie.
    For it's home, dearie, home—it's home I want to be.
    Our topsails are hoisted, and we'll away to sea.
    O, the oak and the ash and the bonnie birken tree
    They're all growing green in the old countrie.

Ballade. (Not to be confused with ballad.) Of all
the French forms, the ballade is not only the oldest but,
by all odds, the most popular. Its origins and history
have been traced in detail by Helen Louise Cohen in her
Lyric Forms from France. In France, it enjoyed its
greatest vogue during the Fourteenth and Fifteenth
Centuries, and although the form was little used for
over two hundred years, interest in it was revived through
the remarkable work of Théodore de Banville (1802–
1891) who brought back to French poetry the intricate
rhyme schemes. In England the ballade, although used as
early as the Fifteenth Century, never came into great
favor until recently. Its popularity may be said to date
from 1877, when Edmund Gosse and Austin Dobson
introduced these involved forms into English verse.
Andrew Lang, W. E. Henley, and A. C. Swinburne
followed suit and by 1890 the ballade and the rondeau
were almost as firmly established as the sonnet. In a
"Note on Some Foreign Forms of Verse," written in
1878, Austin Dobson remarked: "Most of the French
forms are not yet suited for, nor are they intended to

rival the more approved natural rhythms in the treatment of grave and elevated themes. What is modestly advanced for them is that they may add a new charm of buoyancy, a lyric freshness, to amatory and light verse."

The structure of the ballade is extremely strict. It consists of three stanzas of eight (a few examples have ten) lines and another stanza (or half-stanza) of four lines called the *envoy* which, following the old custom, is generally addressed to some prince or imaginary power. The rhymes of the first stanza are arranged in the order *a-b-a-b-b-c-b-c,* and the rhymes as well as the arrangement are repeated in all the others—the envoy (or half-stanza) being *b-c-b-c.* No rhyme-word or rhyming sound may be repeated throughout the entire ballade; thus if the word *light* is used in the first stanza, it cannot be repeated (nor can the word *delight* be used) in any other stanza.

The outstanding feature of the ballade is its *refrain.* The refrain is the line which ends all the stanzas and the envoy. It is thus repeated *in its entirety* and gives a unity to the poem itself. The importance of this (as well as a rhymed explanation of the form itself) has been expressed by a young student in the following example, published in a high-school magazine in 1925.

Ballade on the Ballade

You urge me on; you make me write;	a
In vain your mandates I defy.	b
Yet though the form is like a fight	a
That twists my very thoughts awry,	b
I seize my pen—one can but try	b
And try again and yet again.	c
Still there's one thing I can't deny:	b
Ballades are built on their refrain.	c

First one must make the words contrite   a
    (And here and there insert a sigh).   b
Eight lines times three must one unite   a
    And then an envoy add thereby.   b
    Only three rhymes can one supply,   b
And these without a hint of strain,   c
    Besides (I cannot tell a lie)   b
Ballades are built on their refrain.   c

There must be sense that one can cite,   a
    Besides the form to please the eye.   b
The verse and meter should be light.   a
    A moral too might fortify   b
    The rambling text; the rhymes must vie   b
With resonance. But this is plain,   c
    Though most of them may dim and die,   b
Ballades are built on their refrain.   c

Envoy

Oh Prince, I cannot answer why   b
    (Though I have racked my rocking brain   c
And wrung all reason from it dry)   b
    Ballades are built on their refrain!   c
                —*Richard Untermeyer*

A favorite device of the writers of ballades is the using of a refrain which asks a question. One of the most famous is the *ubi sunt* theme. Villon popularized this in his "*Mais où sont les neiges d'antan?*" Andrew Lang imitated it in the refrain "Nay, but where is the last year's snow?" Other poets asked: "Where are the gods of Yesterday?" "Where are the ships of Tyre?" "Where are the cities of olden time?" etc. One of the best of this type, although the refrain deviates from the strict rule by being slightly varied with each repetition, is the following:

I Wonder in What Isle of Bliss

I wonder in what Isle of Bliss	a
Apollo's music fills the air;	b
In what green valley Artemis	a
For young Endymion spreads the snare;	b
Where Venus lingers debonair;	b
The Wind has blown them all away—	c
And Pan lies piping in his lair—	b
Where are the Gods of Yesterday?	c

Say where the great Semiramis	a
Sleeps in a rose-red tomb; and where	b
The precious dust of Caesar is,	a
Or Cleopatra's golden hair:	b
Where Alexander Do-and-Dare;	b
The Wind has blown them all away—	c
And Redbeard of the Iron Chair:	b
Where are the Dreams of Yesterday?	c

Where is the Queen of Herod's kiss,	a
And Phryne in her beauty bare;	b
By what strange sea does Tomyris	a
With Dido and Cassandra share	b
Divine Proserpina's despair;	b
The Wind has blown them all away—	c
For what poor Ghost does Helen care?	b
Where are the Girls of Yesterday?	c

Envoy

Alas for lovers! Pair by pair	b
The Wind has blown them all away:	c
The young and yare, the fond and fair:	b
Where are the Snows of Yesterday?	c

          —Justin Huntly McCarthy

(It may be noted that the sixth line in each of these verses furnishes an additional refrain.)

The Double Ballade is not to be confused with the ballade à double refrain, but is merely a more extended ballade with double the number of stanzas. The verses themselves usually consist of eight lines, though there are several examples with ten, and one splendid poem (Henley's "Double Ballade of the Nothingness of Things") employs eleven lines, but in every case there are six stanzas. The envoy is optional, and though Swinburne and Henley, both of whom were fond of this extended form, added it to their half-dozen stanzas, most of the other writers discard the envoy.

Owing to the double difficulty of this variation, there are comparatively few authors who have attempted to wrestle with its complexities and it has gone almost entirely out of favor. However, Swinburne's "Double Ballade of August" and Henley's "Double Ballade of Life and Fate" continue to be quoted, and though the following example appears rarely in recent collections it is surely as illuminating as the more familiar ones.

Double Ballade of the Singers of the Time

Why are our songs like the moan of the main,	a
When the wild winds buffet it to and fro,	b
(Our brothers ask us again and again)	a
A weary burden of hopes laid low?	b
Have birds ceased singing or flowers to blow?	b
Is Life cast down from its fair estate?	c
This I answer them—nothing mo'—	b
Songs and singers are out of date.	c

What shall we sing of? Our hearts are fain,	a
Our bosoms burn with a sterile glow.	b
Shall we sing of the sordid strife for gain,	a
For shameful honor, for wealth and woe,	b
Hunger and luxury,—weeds that throw	b
Up from one seeding their flowers of hate?	c
Can we tune our lutes to these themes? Ah no!	b
Songs and singers are out of date.	c

Our songs should be of Faith without stain,   a
    Of haughty honor and deaths that sow   b
The seeds of life on the battle-plain,   a
    Of loves unsullied and eyes that show   b
    The fair white soul in the deeps below.   b
Where are they, these that our songs await   c
    To wake to joyance? Doth any know?   b
Songs and singers are out of date.   c

What have we done with meadow and lane?   a
    Where are the flowers and hawthorn-snow?   b
Acres of brick in the pitiless rain,—   a
    These are our gardens for thorpe and stow!   b
    Summer has left us long ago,   b
Gone to the lands where the turtles mate   c
    And the crickets chirp in the wild-rose row.   b
Songs and singers are out of date.   c

We sit and sing to a world in pain;   a
    Our heartstrings quiver sadly and slow;   b
But, aye and anon, the murmurous strain   a
    Swells up to a clangour of strife and throe,   b
    And the folk that hearken, or friend or foe,   b
Are 'ware that the stress of the time is great   c
    And say to themselves, as they come and go,   b
Songs and singers are out of date.   c

Winter holds us, body and brain: a
    Ice is over our being's flow;   b
Song is a flower that will droop and wane,   a
    If it have no heaven towards which to grow.   b
    Faith and beauty are dead, I trow;   b
Nothing is left but fear and fate: c
    Men are weary of hope; and so   b
Songs and singers are of date.   c

                —*John Payne*

Ballade à Double Refrain. The ballade à double refrain is, as its name suggests, a ballade with *two* re-

frains. One of these refrains occurs in the middle of
each stanza, being repeated in its entirety as the fourth
line of every verse. Both refrains occur in the envoy,
and the charm of the double ballade is its skillful use of
the repetition without letting it become tiresome. In
order to avoid monotony, the two refrains are usually
opposite in character—forming either an actual contra-
diction or a sharp contrast in mood and sentiment. One
of the best known of this type of ballade is the following:

The Ballade of Prose and Rhyme

When the roads are heavy with mire and rut,	a
In November fogs, in December snows,	b
When the North Wind howls, and the doors are shut,	a
There is place and enough for the pains of prose;	b
But whenever a scent from the whitethorn blows,	b
And the jasmine-stars to the casement climb,	c
And a Rosalind-face at the lattice shows,	b
Then hey!—for the ripple of laughing rhyme!	c

When the brain gets dry as an empty nut,	a
And the reason stands on its squarest toes,	b
When the mind (like a beard) has a " formal cut,"	a
There is place and enough for the pains of prose;	b
But whenever the May-blood stirs and glows	b
And the young year draws to the " golden prime,"—	c
And Sir Romeo sticks in his ear a rose,	b
Then hey!—for the ripple of laughing rhyme!	c

In a theme where the thoughts have a pedant-strut	a
In a changing quarrel of " Ayes " and " Noes,"	b
In a starched procession of " If " and " But,"	a
There is place and enough for the pains of prose;	b
But whenever a soft glance softer glows,	b
And the light hours dance to the trysting-time,	c
And the secret is told " that no one knows,"	b
Then hey!—for the ripple of laughing rhyme!	c

Envoy

In the work-a-day world,—for its needs and woes,	b
There is place and enough for the pains of prose;	b
But wherever the May-bells clash and chime,	c
Then hey!—for the ripple of laughing rhyme!	c

—*Austin Dobson*

Blank Verse. Although to most English readers the term has become synonymous with Shakespeare's plays, blank verse is by no means confined to the long un-rhymed line of ten syllables and five accents. Any verse which is without end-rhyme and which usually is not divided into stanzas might be called blank verse—no matter how short the lines or how long the poem itself may be. There are even examples of blank-verse lyrics, of which two are here quoted:

> God on His throne is
> Eldest of poets:
> Unto His measures
>   Moveth the Whole.
>   —*William Watson*

> Now air is hush'd, save where the weak-eyed bat
> With short shrill shriek flits by on leathern wing;
> Or where the beetle winds
> His small but sullen horn.
>
> *To Evening*   —*William Collins*

In spite of the fact that it lends itself to a great many variations, most blank verse, which was introduced into English poetry as early as the Sixteenth Century, is written in an unrhymed five-accented line which is sometimes called "unrhymed heroic" but more frequently *iambic pentameter*. (A reference to the section entitled "A Handbook of Poetic Terms" will show why it was given this name.) Iambic pentameter is the most ma-jestic and resonant of all metrical forms; it is particularly effective when employed in descriptive and dramatic poetry. It is for this reason that the greatest philosophical poets, like Milton and Browning, as well as the greatest dramatists, turned to it instinctively. In the hands of Marlowe and Shakespeare it attained an almost incredible variety, and it is interesting to note how in Shakespeare's later work the form became still more fluent through the use of extra syllables, a device which many of the other Elizabethan playwrights followed.

> Was this the face that launched a thousand ships
> And burnt the topless towers of Ilium?
> *Dr. Faustus*   —*Christopher Marlowe*

> She never told her love,
> But let concealment, like a worm i' the bud,
> Feed on her damask cheek. She pined in thought;
> And, with a green and yellow melancholy,
> She sat like Patience on a monument,
> Smiling at grief. Was this not love, indeed?
> *Twelfth Night*   —*William Shakespeare*

Another type of blank verse which has been made familiar by Longfellow is the unrhymed six-accented verse (*dactylic hexameter*) of "Evangeline." Still another variety is the four-accented unrhymed line with trochaic feet, a form which Longfellow also popularized. A short example is here reprinted.

> Give me of your bark, O Birch-tree!
> Of your yellow bark, O Birch-tree!
> Growing by the rushing river,
> Tall and stately in the valley!
> I a light canoe will build me,
> Build a swift Cheemaun for sailing,
> That shall float upon the river,
> Like a yellow leaf in Autumn,
> Like a yellow water-lily!
> *Hiawatha*   —*Henry Wadsworth Longfellow*

In general, blank verse is a deceptive form for the young writer of poetry; its lack of rhyme and apparent simplicity make it seem the easiest whereas it is actually the most difficult medium to sustain. As Tom Hood, son of the famous poet, once wrote, "It is easy enough to attain the blankness of blank verse—the verse is another matter." The absence of a rhyme pattern necessitates the most perfect harmony if the lines are to be anything beyond prose chopped up into various lengths.

Chant Royal. The *chant royal* is one of the rarer of the French forms, and was so called either from the legend that it was a form selected for composition before the king, or because poets succeeding in the making of chants royal were considered worthy of regal honors. It is actually a larger form of the ballade, consisting of *five* verses of *eleven* lines and an envoy of *five*. In common with all other types of the ballade, the order of the rhymes is the same in every stanza and each verse ends with the same refrain. Twelve examples of the chant royal may be found in Helen Louise Cohen's *Lyric Forms from France* and an excellent burlesque by H. C. Bunner entitled "Behold the Deeds!" is quoted on page 96 of the revised edition of *Modern American Poetry*.

The rhyme order of the chant royal varies somewhat with the different practitioners of this form. Usually, however, it is as follows: *a-b-a-b-c-c-d-d-e-d-e*. The rhymes of the envoy follow in the same order as those in the last five lines, namely *d-d-e-d-e*. In spite of its difficulty, this form has found more favor than the double ballade to which it is related, even such contemporaries as Richard Le Gallienne, Clinton Scollard, and Don Marquis have written in this form. With most of the poets, however, the chant royal begins as an example of skill and remains little more than a *tour de force*. The most famous and by all odds the best chant royal is the one by Austin Dobson, who still must be acknowledged the greatest master of all the French forms:

The Dance Of Death

(*After Holbein*)

"*Contra vim Mortis*
Non est medicamen in hortis."

He is the despots' Despot. All must bide,	a
Later or soon, the message of his might;	b
Princes and potentates their heads must hide,	a
Touched by the awful sigil of his right;	b
Beside the Kaiser he at eve doth wait	c
And pours a potion in his cup of state;	c
The stately Queen his bidding must obey;	d
No keen-eyed Cardinal shall him affray;	d
And to the Dame that wantoneth he saith—	e
"Let be, Sweet-heart, to junket and to play."	d
There is no King more terrible than Death.	e
The lusty Lord, rejoicing in his pride,	a
He draweth down; before the armèd Knight	b
With jangling bridle-rein he still doth ride;	a
He crosseth the strong Captain in the fight;	b
The Burgher grave he beckons from debate;	c
He hales the Abbot by his shaven pate,	c
Nor for the Abbess' wailing will delay;	d
No bawling Mendicant shall say him nay;	d
E'en to the pyx the Priest he followeth,	e
Nor can the Leech his chilling finger stay.	d
There is no King more terrible than Death.	e
All things must bow to him. And woe betide	a
The Wine-bibber, the Roisterer by night;	b
Him the feast-master, many bouts defied,	a
Him 'twixt the pledging and the cup shall smite;	b
Woe to the Lender at usurious rate,	c
The hard Rich Man, the hireling Advocate;	c

Woe to the Judge that selleth right for pay;	d
Woe to the Thief that like a beast of prey	d
With creeping tread the traveller harryeth:—	e
These, in their sin, the sudden sword shall slay.	d
There is no King more terrible than Death.	e

He hath no pity,—nor will be denied.	a
When the low hearth is garnishèd and bright	b
Grimly he flingeth the dim portal wide,	a
And steals the Infant in the Mother's sight;	b
He hath no pity for the scorned of fate:—	c
He spares not Lazarus lying at the gate,	c
Nay, nor the Blind that stumbleth as he may;	d
Nay, the tired Ploughman, at the sinking ray,	d
In the last furrow, feels an icy breath,	e
And knows a hand hath turned the team astray.	d
There is no King more terrible than Death.	e

He hath no pity. For the new-made Bride,	a
Blithe with the promise of her life's delight,	b
That wanders gladly by her Husband's side,	a
He with the clatter of his drum doth fright;	b
He scares the Virgin at the convent grate;	c
The Maid half-won, the Lover passionate;	c
He hath no grace for weakness and decay:	d
The tender Wife, the Widow bent and gray,	d
The feeble Sire whose footsteps faltereth,—	e
All these he leadeth by the lonely way.	d
There is no King more terrible than Death.	e

Envoy

Youth, for whose ear and 'monishing of late,	c
I sang of prodigals and lost estate,	c
Have thou thy joy of living and be gay;	d
But know not less that there must come a day,	d
Aye, and perchance e'en now it hasteneth,	e
When thine own heart shall speak to thee and say,	d
There is no King more terrible than Death!	e

—Austin Dobson

Cinquain. (See **Quintet.**)

Couplet. A couplet (or, as it used to be called, a *distich*) is, as the name implies, a pair of rhymes. To quote the dictionary, it is "two lines of matched verse in immediate succession"—that is, the lines must *match* in length, in rhyme, or both. Here are two different types of couplets in two different meters:

> The apple dangling by an amber clasp
> Provides a golden wardrobe for the wasp.
> > *—Joseph Auslander*

> I sprang to the stirrup, and Joris, and he;
> I galloped, Dirck galloped, we galloped all three.
> > *—Robert Browning*

Browning also furnishes an example of a couplet formed by two lines of irregular length:

> Where the quiet-colored end of evening smiles
> Miles on miles.

Although so short that it rarely stands by itself, a couplet may sometimes constitute a complete though brief poem. Many of the perfect epigrams are, at the same time, perfect couplets, such as Dryden's satirical verse:

> Here lies my wife: here let her lie!
> Now she's at rest—and so am I.

The shortest poem in English—perhaps the shortest poem in any language—is Strickland Gillilan's couplet which he has humorously entitled "Lines on the Antiquity of Microbes." These are the "Lines" in their entirety:

> Adam
> Had 'em.

Distich. (See **Couplet.**)
Double Ballade. (See **Ballade.**)

Five-Line Stanza.   (See **Quintet.**)
Fixed Forms.   (See **French Forms.**)
Four-Line Stanza.   (See **Quatrain.**)
French Forms.   The French forms are so called because they originated in the country of the troubadours,
as early as the Fourteenth Century.   Originally religious in character, the ballades and their kind became
highly popular at court and castle and even the gutters
of Paris echoed with their technical ingenuities when
Villon wrote his immortal refrain, *"Mais où sont les neiges
d'antan?"*   ("But where are the snows of yesterday?")

These forms are also referred to as the fixed forms
because their structures are particularly rigid.   Each
different form has different rules governing its metrical
formation.   But all of them have one rule in regard to
their rhymes: *No word or syllable once used as a rhyme
can be used again throughout the entire poem, not even
if it is spelled differently.*   The rhyming syllable, in each
case, must be a new one in *sound.*   Thus if the word
right is used in the first stanza of any of the French
forms, it cannot be used in any of the other stanzas,
nor can the word *write* or *rite* (which are not rhymes,
but actually the same sound) be used in any part of the
poem.   It is this very limitation of rhyme which makes
the French forms so difficult—and so fascinating.

The ballade is the first of the French forms of which
we have any record; Chaucer wrote several ballades
which are assumed to be the earliest English examples
of this verse form.   Although several other English poets
of the early Fifteenth Century experimented in these
difficult constructions, it was not until the end of the
Nineteenth Century that the French forms were fully
established in England.   It was Austin Dobson, following the French poet Banville, who reintroduced the old

refrain poetry. Dobson and his followers made the French forms a vogue and, though much of the verse-making of the Nineties seems nothing more than the artificial making of verse, the names of some of the most prominent poets of the period are associated with the revival of the French forms. To-day, when one speaks of ballades and rondeaus, one thinks at once not only of Austin Dobson, but of W. E. Henley, Andrew Lang, Edmund Gosse, Richard Le Gallienne, and, possibly first of all, A. C. Swinburne.

Until recently the best collection of this type of poetry was Gleeson White's *Ballades and Rondeaus*. Lately, however, a much more extended compilation as well as a more detailed explanation of the various structures has appeared: Helen Louise Cohen's *Lyric Forms from France*, a volume which is not only a comprehensive anthology, but a work which traces the history of its examples back to their origins.

The most important of the French forms are the ballade, the ballade à double refrain, the rondeau, the rondel, the roundel, the villanelle, and the triolet—all of which are defined, with examples, in this section under the separate alphabetical divisions.

Iambic Pentameter. (See **Blank Verse.**)

Limerick. Frowned on by purists and pedagogues, denied a place in most serious collections, the limerick is, nevertheless, one of the most popular of the lighter forms. It is supposed to derive its name from an Irish song, each verse of which dealt with the adventures of different inhabitants of various villages, the chorus being, "Will you come up to Limerick?" Although several examples of the form exist before 1830, Edward Lear's immortal verses, composed between the years 1832 and 1836 and published in his *Book of Nonsense* in 1846, were the first to draw attention to these ingenious brevities.

Ever since the days of Lear, the limerick has flourished —even among those who are wholly ignorant of poetry. Innumerable newspaper competitions have been held in England and America, hundreds of thousands of "missing last lines" have been supplied by contestants and, it has been estimated, at least one million limericks, good, mediocre, and indecent, are in existence to-day.

The simplicity of the form may account for its widespread favor. It is a five-line stanza built on two rhymes (the rhymes being expressed by the symbol *a-a-b-b-a*) with the third and fourth lines one foot shorter than the other three. Edward Lear's limericks depend on their wildness and fantastic " plots " for their effects. Technically they are not as interesting as the modern limericks; from a rhyming point of view they offer no surprise, for in most cases, the rhyme of the last line is a mere repetition of the first one. The contemporary limerick uses the surprise of a new or curious rhyme as its final twist, often making its point by a freak of spelling or some trick in typographical arrangement. To illustrate the difference, examples of both periods are given. The first three are by Edward Lear.

There was an Old Man who said, " How
Shall I flee from this horrible Cow?
    I will sit on this stile,
    And continue to smile,
Which may soften the heart of that Cow."

❖

There was an Old Man who said, " Hush!
I perceive a young bird in this bush! "
    When they said, " Is it small? "
    He replied, " Not at all;
It is four times as big as the bush! "

> There was a Young Lady of Norway,
> Who casually sat in a doorway;
>   When the door squeezed her flat,
>   She exclaimed, "What of that?"
> This courageous Young Lady of Norway.

The following limerick in the Lear manner is more modern, although its authorship is uncertain:

> There was an old man of Nantucket,
> Who kept all his cash in a bucket;
>   But his daughter, named Nan,
>   Ran away with a man,
> And as for the bucket—Nantucket!

Among the more famous "tricky" limericks—those whose point depends on the humor of spelling or pronunciation—the following are notable:

> There was a young fellow of Gloucester,
> Whose wife ran away with a coucester,[1]
>   He traced her to Leicester,
>   And tried to arreicester,
> But in spite of his efforts he loucester.

❖

> There was a young lady of Warwick,
> Who lived in a castle histarwick,
>   On the damp castle mould
>   She contracted a could,
> And the doctor prescribed paregarwick.

❖

> There was a young person named Tate
> Who went out to dine at 8.8,
>   But I'd hate to relate
>   What that person named Tate
> And his tête-à-tête ate at 8.8.

(The last has been credited to Carolyn Wells.)

---

[1] Coster (or costermonger) is a term applied in England to hawkers and peddlers of fruit.

A limerick which became internationally known was quoted so often by Woodrow Wilson that even so astute an editor as Langford Reed (compiler of *The Complete Limerick Book*) credited the late President with its authorship. This limerick, quoted below, is actually by Anthony Euwer and appeared originally in his *Limeratomy*.

> As a beauty I am not a star,
> There are others more handsome, by far.
>> But my face—I don't mind it
>> For I am behind it.
> It's the people in front that I jar!

Miltonic Sonnet. (See subdivision under **Sonnet** on page 85.)

Octave. In a strict sense, the *octave* is the first eight lines of the sonnet—usually, but not always, separated by a space from the *sestet*, which constitutes the second part of the sonnet.

In a general sense, however, the word octave denotes a verse or stanza of eight lines. Its variety is almost endless. A few of the commoner forms might be listed as follows: the linking together of two ordinary quatrains —expressed by the symbol *a-b-a-b-c-d-c-d* (as in the first example, *sea* formerly being pronounced to rhyme with *survey*); two triplets with a pair of rhyming lines, one after each triplet—expressed by the symbol *a-a-a-b-c-c-c-b* (as in the second example); a combination of a quatrain, a triplet, and an additional rhyme—a form used with great beauty by Swinburne (as in the third example), expressed by the symbol *a-b-a-b-c-c-c-b*.

> I am monarch of all I survey,   a
>> My right there is none to dispute,   b
> From the centre all round to the sea,   a
>> I am lord of the fowl and the brute.   b

O solitude! where are the charms   c
    That sages have seen in thy face?   d
Better dwell in the midst of alarms,   c
    Than reign in this horrible place.   d

Alexander Selkirk   *—William Cowper*

Upon Saint Crispin's Day   a
Fought was this noble fray,   a
Which fame did not delay   a
    To England to carry.   b
O when shall English men   c
With such acts fill a pen?   c
Or England breed again   c
    Such a King Harry?   b

Agincourt   *—Michael Drayton*

From too much love of living,   a
    From hope and fear set free,   b
We thank with brief thanksgiving   a
    Whatever gods may be   b
That no life lives forever;   c
That dead men rise up never;   c
That even the weariest river   c
    Winds somewhere safe to sea.   b

The Garden of Proserpine   *—A. C. Swinburne*

A particular form of the eight-line stanza is known as *ottava rima,* so called since it was taken from the Italian. It may be expressed by the symbols *a-b-a-b-a-b-c-c.* Byron was particularly fond of this variation.

The angels were all singing out of tune,   a
    And hoarse with having little else to do,   b
Excepting to wind up the sun and moon,   a
    Or curb a runaway young star or two,   b
Or wild colt of a comet, which too soon   a
    Broke out of bounds o'er the ethereal blue,   b
Splitting some planet with its playful tail,   c
As boats are sometimes by a wanton whale.   c

The Vision of Judgment   *—Lord Byron*

Ode. The ode, strictly speaking, has no particular form. It may be a short celebration or a long apostrophe; it may be extremely lyrical or gravely philosophical. However, it may be said to be a profound treatment (or a profound attempt to treat) a profound subject. It may *usually* be recognized by its combination of high seriousness and emotional intensity. It is not so much in favor to-day, but the study of classic English poetry reveals more than a score of these extended flights of song. Five of the greatest are undoubtedly Milton's " On the Morning of Christ's Nativity," Wordsworth's " Intimations of Immortality," Shelley's "To a Skylark," Keats's " On a Grecian Urn," and the same writer's " Ode to a Nightingale," the last being possibly the greatest poem of its kind ever written in English.

Ottava Rima. (See **Octave**.)

Pantoum. Although the pantoum may be found in most of the collections of French forms, it is not, strictly speaking, a French form at all. It is of Malay origin and was first popularized by Victor Hugo in his *Orientales*. It is written in four-line stanzas, and each verse repeats intact two of the lines of the preceding verse. To be precise, the *second* and *fourth* line of each stanza become the *first* and *third* of each succeeding one throughout the poem until the end. There is no fixed rule concerning the number of verses which may ensue, but, at the close, the second and fourth line of the *last* stanza are the same as the first and third lines of the *first* stanza— usually reversed, so that the first and last line of the poem are identical. It is the least interesting of the fixed forms and its continual repetition gives it a decided monotony, a monotony which Austin Dobson has used to splendid effect in his pantoum, "In Town," in which the repeated lines convey the constant recurrence of street cries and the insistent buzz of the flies. A more modern example of this form (quoted below) uses the reiterated lines ironically in an effort to reproduce the aimless chatter of a group of *nouveaux riches* at the Opera.

"First Performance"

(Metropolitan Opera House)

" Looks like a big night to-night."
" Here is the rest of the ghetto."
" There she is—there, to the right."
" Heavens! I've lost my libretto!"

" Here is the rest of the ghetto."
" How did they ever get in?"
" Heavens! I've lost my libretto!"
" Hush! It's about to begin!"

" How did they ever get in?"
" Why do they clap for the leader?"
" Hush! It's about to begin!"
" Who sings the part of *Aida?* " [1]

" Why do they clap for the leader?"
" Reginald, *can't* you keep still?"
" Who sings the part of *Aida?*"
" I *know* that I'm going to be ill."

" Reginald, *can't* you keep still?"
" I doubt if they're real; they don't glisten."
" I *know* that I'm going to be ill."
" —*She* said, then *I* said, ' Now, listen—!' "

" I doubt if they're real; they don't glisten."
" That Rossiter's girl's a disgrace!"
" —*She* said, then *I* said, ' Now, listen—!' "
" —and just a *suggestion* of lace."

[1] The pronunciation throughout is New Yorkese.

"That Rossiter's girl's a disgrace."
      "Oh, *no*, Wagner *never* is boring!"
" —and just a *suggestion* of lace."
      "Fred, will you *kindly* stop snoring."

"Oh, *no*, Wagner *never* is boring!"
      "There she is—there, to the right."
"Fred, will you *kindly* stop snoring."
      "Looks like a big night to-night!"
                                    —*Michael Lewis*

Petrarchan Sonnet. (See under **Sonnet** on page 83.)

Pindaric Ode. The name comes from Pindar (*circa* 522–443 B.C.), the great lyric poet of ancient Greece. Referring to this form, the *Encyclopædia Britannica* speaks authoritatively as follows: "The name by which was known a class of loose and irregular odes greatly in fashion in England during the close of the 17th and the beginning of the 18th century. The invention is due to Abraham Cowley, who, . . . perhaps in 1650, found a text of Pindar and determined to imitate the Greek poetry in English, without having comprehended the system upon which Pindar's prosody was built up. Cowley published, however, in 1656, fifteen *Pindarique Odes*, which became the model on which countless imitators founded their pindarics. [Pindar's own odes were extremely regular. *Editor*] . . . The English pindaric was a blunder founded upon a misconception. . . . Although the vogue of these forms hardly survived the age of Anne, something of the vicious tradition of them still remained, and even in the odes of Wordsworth, Shelley and Coleridge the broken versification of Cowley's pindarics occasionally survives. Tennyson's *Ode on the Death of the Duke of Wellington* (1852) is the latest important specimen of a pindaric in English literature."

Quatrain. The quatrain is the most common stanza

structure in all poetry. Although it consists of only four lines, this form is almost endless in its variations and possibilities.

Perhaps the most familiar arrangement is the one which rhymes the first and third, and the second and fourth lines—an arrangement of rhymes which may be expressed by the symbols *a-b-a-b*. Here are five different examples of this most popular type of quatrain—different in beat and length of line:

> By the rude bridge that arched the flood,   a
> Their flag to April's breeze unfurled,   b
> Here once the embattled farmers stood   a
> And fired the shot heard round the world.   b
> —*Ralph Waldo Emerson*

> Throw away thy rod,   a
> Throw away thy wrath,   b
> O my god,   a
> Take the gentle path.   b
> —*George Herbert*

> From you, Ianthe, little troubles pass   a
> Like little ripples down a sunny river;   b
> Your pleasures spring like daisies in the grass,   a
> Cut down and up again as blithe as ever.   b
> —*Walter Savage Landor*

> Whither, O splendid ship, thy white sails crowding,   a
> Leaning across the bosom of the urgent West,   b
> That fearest nor sea rising, nor sky clouding,   a
> Whither away, fair rover, and what thy quest?   b
> —*Robert Bridges*

> Queen, for whose house my fathers fought,   a
> With hopes that rose and fell,   b
> Red star of boyhood's fiery thought,   a
> Farewell.   b
> —*A. C. Swinburne*

Another way of constructing the quatrain is to rhyme only the *second* and *fourth* lines, leaving the first and third *un*rhymed—a form expressed by the symbols *a-b-c-b*. This variation has been condemned as careless and inartistic by many; nevertheless, English poetry is full of examples of this sort. Practically all of the Ballads are constructed of quatrains of this type, two of which are given below:

> It was an ancient Mariner   a
>   And he stoppeth one of three.   b
> " By thy long grey beard and glittering eye,   c
>   Now wherefore stopp'st thou me? "   b
>   —*Samuel Taylor Coleridge*

> Happy, happy time, when the white star hovers   a
>   Low over dim fields fresh with blooming dew,   b
> Near the face of dawn, that draws athwart the darkness,   c
>   Threading it with color, like yewberries the yew.   b
>   —*George Meredith*

Many quatrains have been formed of two couplets— expressed by the symbols *a-a b-b*. Sometimes the couplets are identical in length; often they are varied. Here are three different examples:

> The boys are up in the woods with day   a
> To fetch the daffodils away,   a
> And home at noonday from the hills   b
> They bring no dearth of daffodils.   b
>   —*A. E. Housman*

> As sap foretastes the spring,   a
> As Earth ere blossoming   a
>   Thrills   b
> With far daffodils.   b
>   —*Francis Thompson*

> It will last till men weary of pleasure   a
>   In measure;   a
> It will last till men weary of laughter . . .   b
>   And after!   b
>   —*Austin Dobson*

A less common variety, but one which has been used with great effect by many poets, is the quatrain which has the *first* and *last* lines rhyming together and the two middle lines forming a couplet—a rhyme-arrangement which may be expressed by the symbols *a-b-b-a.* Here are two examples:

See! the lark starts up from his bed in the meadow there,	a
Breaking the gossamer threads and the nets of dew,	b
And flashing a-down the river, a flame of blue!	b
The kingfisher flies like an arrow, and wounds the air.	a

—Oscar Wilde

The living come with grassy tread	a
To read the gravestones on the hill;	b
The graveyard draws the living still,	b
But never any more the dead.	a

—Robert Frost

Though less usual, one frequently finds quatrains written entirely on one rhyme—expressed by the symbol *a-a-a-a.* Here is an example:

The wind flapped loose, the wind was still,	a
Shaken out dead from tree and hill:	a
I had walked on at the wind's will,—	a
I sat now, for the wind was still.	a

—Dante Gabriel Rossetti

Another form which is known to us chiefly through FitzGerald's adaptation of *The Rubáiyát* is the one which has the *first*, *second* and *fourth* lines rhyming together and the third line unrhymed—expressed by the symbol *a-a-b-a.*

The moving finger writes; and, having writ,	a
Moves on; nor all your piety nor wit	a
Shall lure it back to cancel half a line,	b
Nor all your tears wash out a word of it.	a

—Omar Khayyám–FitzGerald

As has been said, the variations are almost innumerable. But one cannot dismiss this form without considering that type of quatrain which maintains its structure as well as its music without the aid of any rhyme. Two such examples (the second using *assonance* instead of rhyme) are:

> The lapping of lake water
> Is like the weeping of women,
> The weeping of ancient women
> Who grieved without rebellion.
>
> —*Jean Starr Untermeyer*

> Leaps the little river and laughs at fetters,
> Through the pebbled channel it flutes and flutters;
> Dances down the rapids where Autumn scatters
> Gold on the waters.
>
> —*Don Marquis*

As in the case of the couplet, certain quatrains have constituted entire poems. Possibly the finest quatrain describing the quatrain is Frank Dempster Sherman's precise cameo:

A Quatrain

> Hark at the lips of this pink whorl of shell
>   And you shall hear the ocean's surge and roar:
> So in the quatrain's measure, written well,
>   A thousand lines shall all be sung in four!

Quintet. A quintet, or, as Adelaide Crapsey called her own variety, a cinquain (from the French *cinque*, meaning five) is a five-line stanza. Its almost endless possibilities of variation both in rhyme and length of line make it a particularly musical stanza. The proportion of rhyme seems to be usually three and two—expressed by the symbol *a-b-a-b-b*. The following three examples illustrate various effects that have been achieved in this fluent stanza form.

Teach me half the gladness   a
    That thy brain must know,   b
Such harmonious madness   a
    From my lips would flow   b
The world should listen then—as I am listening now.   b

To a Skylark   *—Percy Bysshe Shelley*

    Go, lovely Rose!   a
Tell her, that wastes her time and me,   b
    That now she knows,   a
When I resemble her to thee,   b
How sweet and fair she seems to be.   b

Go, Lovely Rose   *—Edmund Waller*

I the grain and the furrow,   a
    The plough-cloven clod   b
And the ploughshare drawn thorough,   a
    The germ and the sod,   b
The deed and the doer, the seed and the sower, the dust
          which is God.   b

Hertha   *—A. C. Swinburne*

Adelaide Crapsey, a modern writer, adapted the five-line stanza to her own purpose and wrote a number of complete poems in "cinquains," a form which she originated. Her five-line stanzas, far from being "free verse," as certain critics have claimed, are the strictest of structures—the lines having, respectively, two, four, six, eight, and two syllables each. One example is reprinted here:

Snow

Look up . . .
From bleakening hills
Blows down the light, first breath
Of wintry wind. . . . Look up, and scent
The snow!

Rime Royal. (See **Septet** on page 77.)

Rispetto. The rispetto is a purely Italian form, consisting of inter-rhyming lines. It is always short and lyrical in character, and though variations exist, the usual length is eight lines divided into two quatrains. As a rule, the first quatrain is built on the rhyme scheme *a-b-a-b* and the second *a-a-b-b*. This form has never become popular in English, although examples of it may be found in the works of A. Mary F. Robinson and Sara Teasdale.

Rispetto

What good is there, ah, me, what good in Love?
　　Since even if you love me, we must part;
And since in either, an' you cared enough,
　　There's but division and a broken heart?

And yet, God knows, to hear you say: My Dear!
I would lie down and stretch me on the bier.
And yet would I, to hear you say: My Own!
With mine own hands drag down the burial stone.
　　　　　　　　　　—A. Mary F. Robinson

Rondeau. The rondeau is, with the ballade, the most popular of the French forms. Closely related to the rondel, it has far more charm and adds a pert sprightliness found in none of the other forms. It is interesting to note how much variety can be achieved by this graceful little model. Many of the rondeaus are full of an airy wit; others are frankly tender; still others, like Dobson's "In After Days," are serious and grave.

The rondeau consists of thirteen lines written throughout on two rhymes, the lines themselves being usually of eight syllables. The refrain of the rondeau is a curious one, being made from the first part (usually the first half) of the first line. (In some cases we find the first word only used as a refrain.) In certain examples, the refrain itself rhymes with the other lines; in the great majority, however, the refrain is unrhymed. It (the refrain) occurs both at the end of the second stanza and at the close of the poem. With *X* to represent the refrain, the order of the rhymes would be *a-a-b-b-a   a-a-b-X   a-a-b-b-a-X*.

The French poet, Voiture, wrote a famous rondeau as an instruction to all rondeau-makers. A skillful English paraphrase, made by Austin Dobson, runs:

> You bid me try, blue eyes, to write
> A rondeau. What!—forthwith—to-night?
>   Reflect. Some skill I have, 'tis true;
>   But thirteen lines—and rhymed on two!
> "Refrain," as well. Ah, hapless plight!
>
> Still, here are five lines—ranged aright.
> These Gallic bonds, I feared, would fright
>   My easy Muse. They did till you—
>   *You* bid me try!
>
> This makes them nine. The port's in sight;
> 'Tis all because your eyes are bright!
>   Now, just a pair to end with 'oo'—
>   When maids command, what can't we do?
> Behold! the rondeau—tasteful, light—
>   You bid me try!

Although most rondeaus are, as has been implied, more adroit than earnest, graceful rather than profound, the form has sometimes been used to express essentially serious themes. Dobson's splendid "In After Days" is well known, and the following spirited expression deserves to be:

A Man Must Live

> A man must live! We justify
> Low shift and trick to treason high,
>   A little vote for a little gold,
>   To a whole senate bought and sold,
> With this self-evident reply.

But is it so? Pray tell me why
Life at such cost you have to buy?
    In what religion were you told
        "A man must live"?

There are times when a man must die.
Imagine for a battle-cry
    From soldier with a sword to hold—
    From soldiers with the flag unrolled—
This coward's whine, this liar's lie,
        "A man must live"?
        —*Charlotte Perkins Stetson Gilman*

It is at once evident that the refrain (or repetition of the opening phrase) not only forms an inseparable part of each stanza but is also the climax of the rondeau. Many poets have given this refrain a humorous twist by punning, thus giving the words a new meaning with each repetition. However, though the spelling may be changed or the actual words altered, the *sound* of the refrain must reappear *exactly* in each case. Thus a rondeau may be built on a refrain which appears the first time as " immortal eyes," the second time as " immortal lies," and the third time as " immortalize "! A certain paraphrase of Horace begins by quoting the first phrase of one of the odes in Latin and the refrain of the rondeau appears in this order: " *Cum tu, Lydia*," " Come to Lydia," and " Come to! Lydia! " A well known writer of light verse begins a rondeau " 'Tis Labor Day " and, after rambling through the thirteen lines, ends his poem apologetically with " 'Tis labored—Eh? "

An extremely neat instance of a rondeau with a punning refrain is the following:

A Song to One

If few are won to read my lays
And offer me a word of praise,

        If there are only one or two
        To take my rhymes and read them through,
    I may not claim the poet's bays.

    I care not, when my Fancy plays
    Its one sweet note, if it should raise
        A host of listeners or few—
            If you are one.

    The homage that my full heart pays
    To Womanhood in divers ways,
        Begins and ends, my love, in you.
        My lines may halt, but strong and true
    My soul shall sing through all its days,
            If you are won.   —*T. A. Daly*

Another example of this type, beginning as an amorous
tribute and ending in burlesque, is the following:

    My lady's eyes are fire and jet,
    A dark allure, a laughing threat;
        Her coiled hair is a living mass
        Of copper strands and burnished brass,
    Holding men's hearts in that bright net.

    Her mouth is Beauty's epithet
    Phrased in a double rhyme. And yet
        I do not love her—so, alas,
            My lady sighs.

    How can I? Much to my regret
    I have beheld her silhouette
        Blot out a haystack, cows, a class
        Of little girls who tried to pass. . . .
    Love her? I would—could I forget
            My lady's size.
                        —*Michael Lewis*

The much quoted rondeau of Leigh Hunt is a charming poem which has well deserved its fame. It is, however, not a rondeau in any sense, its only resemblance
being the fact that its first and last phrases are the same.

For those readers who may have forgotten it and as an
extreme variation of the form, it is quoted here:

> Jenny kissed me when we met,
>> Jumping from the chair she sat in;
> Time, you thief, who love to get
>> Sweets into your list, put *that* in:
> Say I'm weary, say I'm sad,
>> Say that health and wealth have missed me,
> Say I'm growing old, but add,
>> Jenny kissed me!

Although most readers are not aware of the fact, the
most widely quoted poem produced by the war, "In
Flanders Fields," by John McCrae, is a rondeau.

Rondeau Redoublé.   The rondeau redoublé is not, as
its name suggests, a double rondeau.   It is actually nothing more than six quatrains, rhyming on two alternating
rhymes, and as a finale, the first *half* of the first line is
used *after* the last (and extra) quatrain.   Its chief feature
is this: Each line of the first quatrain is used *in its entirety* as the last line of each succeeding verse—that is, the
first line of the poem acts as the last line of the *second*
stanza, the *second* line of the poem acts as the last line
of the *third* stanza, and so on.   The first four lines, therefore, act as a kind of text on which the rest of the poem is
built, as may be seen from the following version of Ode
26, Book I, by Horace.

> The Muses love me, and I am content;
>> What are the shades of earth that I should fear?
> The winds will sweep them into banishment,
>> The sea will drag them to an emerald bier.
>
> Let others quail and, trembling, force the tear,
>> And cringe, with looks that on the ground are bent;
> Let all the angry powers of air appear,
>> *The Muses love me—and I am content.*

What though no joy is given but only lent,
　　What though the skies are overcast and drear;
I care not if the thundering heavens are rent—
　　What are the shades of earth that I should fear?

Come then, wave-hearted nymph from brooklets clear,
　　Laughing at greater songs, you need not vent
Your proud disdain upon my verses here;
　　The winds will sweep them into banishment.

O come, with perfumed words from Venus sent,
　　And twine a golden couplet for our cheer.
(Mind not the cares that mar our merriment;
　　The sea will drag them to an emerald bier.)

Attune my strings, and so, for many a year,
　　Singing of thee I will be diligent;
And even when the leaves of life are sere,
　　　　One thought will cheer me when all else is spent:
　　　　The Muses love me.
　　　　　　　　—*Louis Untermeyer*

Rondel. The rondel is the early form of the rondeau
and was largely used in the Fourteenth Century. It is
actually a cross between the rondeau and the triolet,
being possibly more related to the latter since it repeats
some of its lines *in their entirety.* The rhymes (which, in
common with all other French Forms, cannot be repeated)
are only two and are placed in the following order: *A-B-
b-a a-b-A-B a-b-b-a-A.* (The capitals indicate that the
entire line is repeated intact.)

The rondel has several variations which need not de-
tain us, the best type being exemplified by the following:

The Wanderer

Love comes back to his vacant dwelling,—
　　The old, old Love that we knew of yore!
　　We see him stand by the open door,
With his great eyes sad, and his bosom swelling.

He makes as though in our arms repelling,
   He fain would lie as he lay before;—
Love comes back to his vacant dwelling,—
   The old, old Love that we knew of yore!

Ah, who shall help us from over-spelling
   That sweet, forgotten, forbidden lore!
   E'en as we doubt in our heart once more,
With a rush of tears to our eyelids welling,
Love comes back to his vacant dwelling.
                  —*Austin Dobson*

Roundel. The roundel is a slight but extremely interesting variation of the rondeau which was invented by Swinburne. One or two old French poems bear a resemblance to this form, but Swinburne must be given credit not only for its introduction but for the remarkable use he made of it. He wrote one hundred of these experiments (a volume entitled *A Century of Roundels*) of extreme skill and delicacy. The roundel has always eleven lines—two of the lines being the refrain. The rhymes, with *X* as the refrain, are arranged: *a-b-a-X b-a-b a-b-a-X*. In almost every case, the refrain (*X*) rhymes with the *b*-lines. An excellent example as well as a description of the form itself is the following:

The Roundel

A roundel is wrought as a ring or a star-bright sphere,
With craft of delight and with cunning of sound unsought,
That the heart of the hearer may smile if to pleasure his ear
          A roundel is wrought.

Its jewel of music is carven of all or of aught—
Love, laughter or mourning—remembrance of rapture or fear—
That fancy may fashion to hang in the ear of thought.

As a bird's quick song runs round, and the hearts in us hear
Pause answer to pause, and again the same strain caught,

So moves the device whence, round as a pearl or a tear,
   A roundel is wrought.
       —*A. C. Swinburne*

Septet. The septet, or seven-line stanza, is rather uncommon, but it has been used by many poets with subtle variations. Like the sestet, the possibilities of combination are innumerable—in fact there are so many that a list of them would look more like a geometrical problem than a poetic explanation.

One particular variation has been popular ever since the days of Chaucer, who used it with consumate skill in *The Parlement of Foules* and in many of *The Canterbury Tales*. This form is the *rime royal* (so called as it is supposed to owe its origin to the fact that it was first employed by King James I), a seven-line stanza in which the rhymes may be expressed by the symbol *a-b a b b c-c*.

In Surrie whylom [1] dwelte a companye	a
Of chapmen [2] riche, and ther to sadde and trewe,	b
That wyde-wher [3] senten her spycerye,[4]	a
Clothes of gold, and satins riche of hewe;	b
Her chaffar [5] was so thrifty and so newe,	b
That every wight [6] hath deyntee [7] to chaffare	c
With hem,[8] and eek [9] to sellen him hir ware.	c

The Tale of the Man of Law   —*Geoffrey Chaucer*

In our own times, rime royal has been used most consistently and brilliantly by John Masefield, whose narratives echo the vitality of Chaucer. Two of Masefield's finest poems, *The Widow in the Bye Street* and *Dauber* are written in this measure. The following is the opening stanza of the latter long poem:

[1] **whylom,** formerly, once
[2] **chapman,** traders, merchants
[3] **wyde-wher,** widely
[4] **spycerye,** spices
[5] **chaffar,** merchandise (noun), to trade (verb)
[6] **wight,** Creature, person
[7] **deyntee,** delight, pleasure
[8] **hem,** him
[9] **eek,** also

Four bells were struck, the watch was called on deck,	a
All work aboard was over for the hour,	b
And some men sang and others played at check,	a
Or mended clothes or watched the sunset glower.	b
The bursting west was like an opening flower,	b
And one man watched it till the light was dim,	c
But no one went across to talk to him.	c

The following example of a seven-line stanza is quite unlike the rime royal, being constructed entirely on two rhymes:

This is the spray the bird clung to	a
Making it blossom with pleasure	b
Ere the high tree-top she sprung to,	a
Fit for her nest and her treasure.	b
Oh, what a hope beyond measure	a
Was the poor spray's, which the flying feet hung to,—	b
So to be singled out, built in, and sung to.	b

Misconceptions   —*Robert Browning*

Sestet. In its strictest sense, the sestet is the last six lines of a sonnet. It is the second part of the sonnet, usually separated from the first eight lines (the octave) by a space.

In a general sense, it can mean any six-line stanza. This six-line stanza can be written in a hundred different ways—with the increased number of lines it has many more possibilities of variation than the quatrain or quintet. It may be formed by the combination of three couplets—expressed by the symbols *a-a-b-b-c-c;* by a quatrain with an added couplet—expressed by the symbols *a-b-a-b-c-c;* by six lines rhyming alternately—expressed by the symbols *a-b-a-b-a-b;* by the combination of two couplets with an additional pair of rhymes, one line coming after the first couplet, and the other after the second couplet—expressed by the symbols *a-a-b a-a-b*—and dozens of other combinations. The following few ex-

amples, all from well known poems, illustrate the great
variety of which this form is capable:

And if I should live to be	a
The last leaf upon the tree	a
In the spring,	b
Let them smile, as I do now,	c
At the old forsaken bough	c
Where I cling.	b

The Last Leaf   —*Oliver Wendell Holmes*

Fear no more the heat o' the sun,	a
Nor the furious winter's rages;	b
Thou thy worldly task hast done,	a
Home art gone, and ta'en thy wages:	b
Golden lads and girls all must,	c
As chimney-sweepers, come to dust.	c

Cymbeline   —*William Shakespeare*

Love winged my Hopes and taught me how to fly	a
Far from base earth, but not to mount too high:	a
For true pleasure	b
Lives in measure,	b
Which if men forsake,	c
Blinded they into folly run and grief for pleasure take.	c

Second Look of Airs (1601)   —*Robert Jones* (?)

The following form is associated with Robert Burns,
since he used it so often as to make it his own:

In this lone cave, in garments lowly,	a
Alike a foe to noisy folly,	a
And brow-bent gloomy melancholy,	a
I wear away	b
My life, and in my office holy,	a
Consume the day.	b

The Hermit   —*Robert Burns*

Sestina. The sestina is, by all odds, the most complicated of the French forms. It is so lengthy and its technical construction is so involved that it is almost impossi-

ble to condense an outline of its construction here. Suffice it to say that the sestina is composed of six stanzas of six lines each, the lines of the six verses ending with *the same six words*, and the arrangement of these six terminal words following a definite and extremely complicated rule. To make the matter still more difficult, there is a final stanza of three lines in which *all* of the six words must be used, three at the ends and three in the middle of the lines. As may be imagined, the form is so intricate that most of the poems in this form are nothing more than technical exercises. However, Rudyard Kipling's "Sestina of the Tramp-Royal" is not only a particularly successful example, but a splendid poem in its own right, and Swinburne, for whom no form was complex enough, actually wrote a double sestina of twelve verses of twelve lines each—revolving through all its one hundred and fifty lines (there is a six-line envoy) on twelve words!

The reader who is sufficiently interested to pursue his studies to the source, will find nine excellent examples in Helen Louise Cohen's *Lyric Forms from France* and a complete analysis (as well as half a dozen illustrative sestinas) in Gleeson White's condensed *Ballades and Rondeaus*.

White, realizing the intricacy of this form, admits that "if the rules themselves are compressed, a more complex and incomprehensible jargon of firsts and seconds and thirds, etc., could hardly be found. The first verse has, of course, the initial order, 1, 2, 3, 4, 5, 6; the second, 6, 1, 5, 2, 4, 3; the third, 3, 6, 4, 1, 2, 5; the fourth, 5, 3, 2, 6, 1, 4; the fifth, 4, 5, 1, 3, 6, 2; the sixth 2, 4, 6, 5, 3, 1; the last half-stanza ends with 2, 4, 6, and uses 1, 3, 5 at the beginning (not the first word always) of the line, or at the half-line in rhymes that permit their introduction there. It will be seen that no end-word occurs more than once in the same place, and that the end-word of every stanza is *invariably* chosen to take its place as terminal of the first line of the next verse."

Although, as has been said, the most famous sestinas have been written by Swinburne, Edmund Gosse and Kipling have similarly excelled in the form (there is also an excellent "Sestina: Altaforte" by Ezra Pound), and James Branch Cabell, known to contemporary readers as the author of a series of brilliantly colored novels, has composed a volume of verse (*From the Hidden Way*) rich in the French Forms, among which the following sestina is one of the best:

The Conqueror Passes

Awaken! for the servitors of Spring
Proclaim his triumph! ah, make haste to see
With what tempestuous pageantry they bring
The victor homeward! Haste, for this is he
That cast out Winter, and all woes that cling
To Winter's garments, and bade April be!

And now that Spring is master, let us be
Content, and laugh as anciently in spring
The battle-wearied Tristram laughed, when he
Was come again Tintagel-ward, to bring
Glad news of Arthur's victory—and see
Ysoude, with parted lips, that waver and cling.

Not yet in Brittany must Tristram cling
To this or that sad memory, and be
Alone, as she in Cornwall; for in spring
Love sows against far harvestings,—and he
Is blind, and scatters baleful seed that bring
Such fruitage as blind Love lacks eyes to see.

Love sows, but lovers reap: and ye will see
The loved eyes lighten, feel the loved lips cling,
Never again when in the grave ye be

Incurious of your happiness in spring,
And get no grace of Love there, whither he
That bartered life for love no love may bring.

No braggart Heracles avails to bring
Alcestis hence; nor here may Roland see
The eyes of Aude; nor here the wakening spring
Vex any man with memories: for there be
No memories that cling as cerements cling,
No force that baffles Death, more strong than he.

Us hath he noted, and for us hath he
An hour appointed; and that hour will bring
Oblivion.—Then laugh! Laugh, dear, and see
The tyrant mocked, while yet our bosoms cling,
While yet our lips obey us, and we be
Untrammeled in our little hour of spring!

Thus in the spring we jeer at Death, though he
Will see our children perish, and will bring
Asunder all that cling while love may be.
                                    —*James Branch Cabell*

Seven-Line Stanza. (See **Septet** on page 77.)
Six-Line Stanza. (See **Sestet** on page 78.)
Sonnet. Although there are many variations of this form, a sonnet is a poem of fourteen lines divided into two parts—the first eight lines being known as the *octave* and the second six lines known as the *sestet.* The sonnet is of Italian origin, and the lightness of the Italian and Spanish speech enabled the poets of the Latin languages to express every phase of grace and gallantry through this medium. In England, however, its structure has made it more suitable for serious and meditative subjects.

In *Sonnets of This Century*, William Sharp lists five formal types: (1) the Petrarchan, (2) the Spenserian, (3) the Shakespearean, (4) the Miltonic, and (5) the contemporary. If one wished to make a separate classification for every variety of sonnet, one could invent more than a dozen other divisions. For the purpose of simplification, however, sonnets may be divided into three general types: (1) the Petrarchan (or Italian) sonnet, (2) the Shakespearean sonnet, and (3) the Miltonic (or unbroken) sonnet.

The Petrarchan sonnet (named after the Italian poet, Petrarch) is the strictest of all: it permits only two rhyme-sounds in the octave and three in the sestet. The perfect Petrarchan octave consists of two quatrains in which the eight lines have a rhyme arrangement which might be expressed by the symbols *a-b-b-a-a-b-b-a*. The sestet has either the rhyme arrangement *a-b-c-a-b-c* or *a-b-a-b-a-b*—most of the Petrarchan models following the former arrangement.

Longfellow has written many sonnets in the pure Petrarchan style, a frequently quoted example being the following one:

Nature

As a fond mother, when the day is o'er	a
Leads by the hand her little child to bed,	b
Half willing, half reluctant to be led	b
And leave his broken playthings on the floor,	a
Still gazing at them through the open door,	a
Nor wholly reassured and comforted	b
By promises of others in their stead,	b
Which, though more splendid, may not please him more;	a
So Nature deals with us, and takes away	c
Our playthings one by one, and by the hand	d
Leads us to rest so gently that we go	e
Scarce knowing if we wish to go or stay,	c
Being too full of sleep to understand	d
How far the unknown transcends the what we know.	e

—*Henry Wadsworth Longfellow*

Another excellent sonnet of this type, in which, however, the rhyme-scheme of the sestet is not Petrarchan in form but Shakespearean, is the one, written in 1828, to which the English poet White owes his entire reputation:

Mysterious Night! when our first parent knew	a
Thee from report divine, and heard thy name,	b
Did he not tremble for this lovely frame,	b
This glorious canopy of light and blue?	a
Yet 'neath a curtain of translucent dew,	a
Bathed in the rays of the great setting flame,	b
Hesperus with the host of heaven came,	b
And lo! Creation widened in man's view.	a
Who could have thought such darkness lay concealed	c
Within thy beams, O Sun! or who could find,	d
Whilst flower and leaf and insect stood revealed,	c
That to such countless orbs thou mad'st us blind!	d
Why do we then shun Death with anxious strife?	e
If Light can thus deceive, wherefore not Life?	e

To Night   —*Joseph Blanco White*

The Shakespearean Sonnet is so called, not because Shakespeare invented it, but because he made so splendid a use of a model in which previous English poets had already experimented. The Shakespearean sonnet completely departs from the interknit Italian type. Instead of having octave and sestet sharply differentiated in rhyme arrangement, it is merely made up of three quatrains concluded by a couplet with a new rhyme. Its formula may be expressed thus: *a-b-a-b c-d-c-d e-f-e-f g-g*. Comparing the two forms, Sharp wrote: " The Shakespearean sonnet is like a red-hot bar being moulded upon a forge till—in the closing couplet—it receives a final clinching blow from the hammer; the Petrarchan sonnet, on the other hand, is like a wind, gathering in volume and dying away again immediately upon attaining its culminating force."

It is difficult to choose an example of the Shakespearean

sonnet; Shakespeare's own sequence contains many of the
most exquisite sonnets in any form and in any language:

Full many a glorious morning have I seen	a
Flatter the mountain tops with sovereign eye,	b
Kissing with golden face the meadows green,	a
Gilding pale streams with heavenly alchemy;	b
Anon permit the basest clouds to ride	c
With ugly rack on his celestial face,	d
And from the forlorn world his visage hide,	c
Stealing unseen to west with this disgrace.	d
Even so my sun one early morn did shine	e
With all-triumphant splendour on my brow;	f
But out, alack! he was but one hour mine;	e
The region-cloud hath masked him from me now.	f
Yet him for this my love no whit disdaineth;	g
Suns of the world may stain, when heaven's sun staineth.	g

Sonnet XXXIII   *—William Shakespeare*

The Miltonic Sonnet was actually invented by Milton; in
his hands, as Wordsworth wrote, it " became a trumpet."
Milton recognized the rhythmical charm of the Petrarchian
sonnet, but he disregarded the break between the octave
and the sestet. Previous to this, most of the sonneteers
divided the thought of their poem into two parts; the
octave usually presented a general idea, while the sestet
made the thought concrete by applying it to some particular person or event. Milton made his sonnets a complete unit, a gradual culmination, rather than the contrast of two ideas. There exist few finer sonnets in the
English language than his own poem on his blindness.

When I consider how my light is spent	a
Ere half my days in this dark world and wide,	b
And that one talent, which is death to hide,	b
Lodged with me useless, though my soul more bent	a
To serve therewith my Maker, and present	a

My true account, lest He, returning, chide;   b
"Doth God exact day-labor, light denied?"   b
I fondly ask.   But Patience, to prevent   a
That murmur, soon replies, "God doth not need   ·   c
Either man's work or His own gifts; who best   d
Bear His mild yoke, they serve Him best.   His state   e
Is kingly; thousands at His bidding speed,   c
And post o'er land and ocean without rest;   d
They also serve who only stand and wait."   e
On His Blindness   —*John Milton*

In connection with this it may be interesting to quote
Wordsworth's own tribute to the sonnet itself, which is,
incidentally, a combination of the Shakespearean and
Miltonic form.   (Tasso was an Italian epic poet of the
Sixteenth Century; Camoëns a Portuguese poet of the
same period.)

Scorn not the Sonnet. Critic, you have frowned,   a
Mindless of its just honours; with this key   b
Shakespeare unlocked his heart; the melody   b
Of this small lute gave ease to Petrarch's wound;   a
A thousand times this pipe did Tasso sound;   a
With it Camoëns soothed an exile's grief;   c
The Sonnet glittered a gay myrtle leaf   c
Amid the cypress with which Dante crowned   b
His visionary brow: a glow-worm lamp,   d
It cheered mild Spenser, called from Faery-land   e
To struggle through dark ways; and, when a damp   d
Fell round the path of Milton, in his hand   e
The thing became a trumpet; whence he blew   f
Soul-animating strains—alas, too few!   f
The Sonnet   —*William Wordsworth*

As every reader knows, one of the most famous poems
in literature is also one of the greatest sonnets.   It is
Keats's "On First Looking into Chapman's Homer"
and is a superb example of the true Petrarchan model.

Much have I travell'd in the realms of gold,   a
    And many goodly states and kingdoms seen;   b
    Round many western islands have I been   b
Which bards in fealty to Apollo hold.   a
Oft of one wide expense had I been told   a
    That deep-brow'd Homer ruled as his demesne;   b
    Yet did I never breathe its pure serene   b
Till I heard Chapman speak out loud and bold: a

Then felt I like some watcher of the skies   c
    When a new planet swims into his ken;   d
Or like stout Cortez when with eagle eyes   c
    He stared at the Pacific—and all his men   d
Look'd at each other with a wild surmise—   c
    Silent, upon a peak in Darien.   d

                  —*John Keats*

Sonnet literature is full of variations of the form, variations in spirit rather than in structure. Many tricks have been attempted in the effort to give the fourteen lines a new piquancy and even to disguise the form itself. One of the most amusing of these is Dobson's sonnet which is given below:

A Sonnet in Dialogue

Frank (on the lawn)
Come to the terrace, May,—the sun is low.

May (in the house)
Thanks, I prefer my Browning here instead.

Frank
There are two peaches by the strawberry bed.

May
They will be riper if we let them grow.

Frank
Then the Park-aloe is in bloom, you know.

May
Also, her Majesty Queen Anne is dead.

Frank
But surely, May, your pony must be fed.

May
And was, and is.　I fed him hours ago.
It's useless, Frank, you see I shall not stir.

Frank
Still, I had something you would like to hear.

May
No doubt some new frivolity of men.

Frank
Nay,—'tis a thing the gentler sex deplores
Chiefly, I think . . .

May (coming to the window)
　　　　　　What is this secret then?

Frank (mysteriously)
There are no eyes more beautiful than yours.
　　　　　　　　　　—Austin Dobson

No reference, however brief, to the sonnet could be complete without mention of the many sonnet sequences which have enriched literature.　These groups of inter-related sonnets form sometimes a narrative, sometimes an exposition of character; more often, however, they are purely a set of associated poems in which the "plot" is less important than the range of emotion.　Critics have differed in their choice of these, although most of them unite in awarding first place to Shakespeare's group of one hundred and fifty-four.　After Shakespeare's im-mortal series, readers have been divided in their affec-tions, but there can be little doubt that a great majority would select the early Philip Sidney's "Astrophel to

Stella " and Spenser's "Amoretti " as the leading sonnet sequences prior to Shakespeare. The two greatest examples of the "linkèd sonnet chain " of the Victorian era are Mrs. Elizabeth Barrett Browning's "Sonnets from the Portuguese" and Dante Gabriel Rossetti's "House of Life."

In America, the form has been less popular, although two remarkable sequences have appeared: Arthur Davison Ficke's " Sonnets of a Portrait Painter," and William Ellery Leonard's autobiographical "Two Lives." It might be added that two American sonneteers, Edna St. Vincent Millay and Edwin Arlington Robinson, have produced some of the most exquisite sonnets of the last half-century, but none of them (except a short group by Miss Millay) constitute a sequence.

Burlesques of the sonnet have existed since the very inception of the form. The ease with which it lends itself to memorial verse has been lampooned by many poets. Among the examples which parody the dedicatory or "pompously purple" sonnet, this is a satirical skeleton:

To ———

O thou	birth
Great	land,
Stern	command
Wisdom	mirth.
Noble	worth,
Future	planned,
All men	understand
Throughout	earth.
Inscrutably	designed,
Glorious	sea to sea;
Foes	blind
Nations	free—
Lover	mankind,
Thy fame	eternity!

—Louis Untermeyer

Although there is no rule as to the *length* of each line in the sonnet, the great majority of sonnets are written in lines of ten syllables (five-foot, or pentameter lines). Once in a while we meet with sonnets of only eight or even six syllables—the paring-down process having reached its limit in the following clever freak, constructed entirely on fourteen lines of one syllable each:

The Aëronaut to His Lady

I	a
Through	b
Blue	b
Sky	a
Fly	a
To	b
You.	b
Why?	a
Sweet	c
Love,	d
Feet	c
Move	d
So	e
Slow!	e

—F. S. (*Frank Sidgwick*)

Spenserian Stanza. The Spenserian stanza, named after Edmund Spenser, who, by his use of it in the Sixteenth Century in *The Faerie Queen*, gave it lasting fame, is a nine-line stanza which moves with unusual pomp and solemnity. Its rhyme scheme is the same as that of the first nine lines of the Spenserian sonnet—and may be expressed by the symbol *a-b-a-b-b-c-b-c-c*. The ninth line (called the Alexandrine) is slightly longer and rounds out the stanza with a rich sonorous ending. Although the Spenserian stanza is in disfavor at present, some of the greatest poems of the past have been written in this form. Among the poets of the Nineteenth Century who employed it, the two most memorable are Byron and Keats. The three examples which follow illustrate differences in idiom between the Sixteenth and the Nineteenth Century and also reveal how differently three poets can express themselves though all three are using the same form.

> For take thy balance, if thou be so wise,
> And weigh the wind that under heaven doth blow;
> Or weigh the light that in the east doth rise;
> Or weigh the thought that from man's mind doth flow:
> But if the weight of these thou canst not show,
> Weigh but one word which from thy lips doth fall:
> For how canst thou these greater secrets know
> That doest not know the least thing of them all?
> Ill can he rule the great that cannot reach the small.

The Faerie Queen   —*Edmund Spenser*

> Roll on, thou deep and dark blue Ocean—roll!
> Ten thousand fleets sweep over thee in vain;
> Man marks the earth with ruin—his control
> Stops with the shore;—upon the watery plain
> The wrecks are all thy deed, nor doth remain
> A shadow of man's ravage, save his own,
> When for a moment, like a drop of rain,
> He sinks into thy depths with bubbling groan,
> Without a grave, unknell'd, uncoffin'd, and unknown.

Childe Harold   —*Lord Byron*

> "Hark! 'tis an elfin-storm from faery land,
> Of haggard seeming, but a boon indeed:
> Arise—arise! The morning is at hand;
> The bloated wassailers will never heed.
> Let us away, my love, with happy speed;
> There are no ears to hear, or eyes to see,—
> Drown'd all in Rhenish and the sleepy mead:
> Awake! arise! my love, and fearless be,
> For o'er the southern moors I have a home for thee."

The Eve of St. Agnes   —*John Keats*

Tercet. (See **Triplet** on page 94.)

Terza Rima. A poem in *terza rima* (" third rhyme ") consists of a set of stanzas of three lines (usually eleven syllables in length) linked in succession by the interlocking of their rhymes: *aba, bcb, cdc, ded, efe,* etc. Although *terza rima* existed before Dante (it is not even certain whether its origin was Italian), his *Divine Comedy* was the work which raised the form from the rank of fluent verses and folk-song to the heights of eloquent austerity.

Terza rima has been used but rarely in English poetry, the most successful employment of it being Mrs. Browning's *Casa Guido Windows* and Shelley's magnificent *Ode to the West Wind.* The *Ode* begins:

> O wild West Wind, thou breath of Autumn's being,
>   Thou from whose unseen presence the leaves dead
> Are driven, like ghosts from an enchanter fleeing,
>
>   Yellow, and black, and pale, and hectic red,
> Pestilence-stricken multitudes! O thou
>   Who chariotest to their dark wintry bed
>
> The wingèd seeds, where they lie cold and low,
>   Each like a corpse within its grave, until
> Thine azure sister of the Spring shall blow
>
>   Her clarion o'er the dreaming earth, and fill
> (Driving sweet buds like flocks to feed in air)
>   With living hues and odors plain and hill;
>
> Wild Spirit, which art moving everywhere;
> Destroyer and preserver; hear, O hear!

Three Line Stanza. (See **Triplet** on page 94.)

Triolet. The triolet is one of the neatest of the French forms. It is a single stanza of eight lines with only two rhymes—the first line being repeated *in its entirety* as the fourth, and the first and second lines being repeated *in their entirety* as the seventh and eighth lines. If the smaller italics represent rhymes and the capital letters stand for lines, the formula for a triolet would be:

$$A\text{-}B\text{-}a\text{-}A\text{-}a\text{-}b\text{-}A\text{-}B.$$

It can be seen that the triolet is not adapted for any profound emotion; its point lies in its grace and skillful turn of phrase. The best triolets are not only ingenious, but, as one poet has put it, " nothing can be more playfully sly than this tiny trill of epigrammatic melody turning so simply upon its own axis."

> Easy is the Triolet,
>   If you really learn to make it!
> Once a neat refrain you get,
> Easy is the Triolet.
> As you see!—I pay my debt
>   With another rhyme. Deuce take it,
> Easy is the Triolet,
>   If you really learn to make it!
> —*W. E. Henley*

Another example, in which the triolet itself is epitomized and punned upon, is the following:

> Heaven bless the Triolet,
>   Short and sweet, that's all.
> Fragile as a violet,
> Heaven bless thee, Triolet.
> Angels from the sky, oh let
>   Blessings on thee fall.
> Heaven bless the Triolet.
> Short and sweet. . . .
>   That's all!
> —*Michael Lewis*

Triplet. A triplet, or as it is sometimes called, a *tercet*, is any stanza of three lines rhyming together. Here are four triplets in varying lengths and different meters.

> Boot, saddle, to horse, and away!
> Rescue my castle before the hot day
> Brightens to blue from its silvery gray.
> —*Robert Browning*

> But John P.
> Robinson, he
> Sez he wunt vote fer Guverner B.
> —*James Russell Lowell*

> There I plucked a faint wild rose
> Hard by where the linden grows
> Sighing over silver rows.
> —*William Morris*

> Whoe'er she be—
> That not impossible she
> That shall command her heart and me.
> —*Richard Crashaw*

Another example of the tercet is quoted under *Monometer*—the poem by Herrick.

Villanelle. The villanelle, in its early form, was a sort of shepherd's song and ever since its origin has been used almost entirely for pastoral subjects or idyllic effects. Though it seems simple, its simplicity is highly artificial, as may be seen from the structure. The villanelle is written in five three-line stanzas and ends with a stanza of four lines, the refrain forming *eight* of the nineteen lines. This repetition is an alternating double refrain, being taken from the first and third lines of the first stanza; the two lines forming alternately the last lines of all the stanzas except the final one. In the last, *both* lines appear together, concluding the couplet. Only two rhymes are permitted throughout the verses.

Henley has described the very essence of the villanelle in his use of it, as follows:

The Villanelle

A dainty thing's the Villanelle.
　　Sly, musical, a jewel in rhyme,
It serves its purpose passing well.

A double-clappered silver bell
　　That must be made to clink in chime,
A dainty thing's the Villanelle;

And if you wish to flute a spell,
　　Or ask a meeting 'neath the lime,
It serves its purpose passing well.

You must not ask of it the swell
　　Of organs grandiose and sublime—
A dainty thing's the Villanelle;

And, filled with sweetness, as a shell
　　Is filled with sound, and launched in time,
It serves its purpose passing well.

Still fair to see and good to smell
　　As in the quaintness of its prime,
A dainty thing's the Villanelle,
It serves its purpose passing well.
　　　　　　　　　　　—*W. E. Henley*

The villanelle, like the triolet, is not usually employed for serious effects, although one of the best modern villanelles is the grave and eerie " The House on the Hill " by Edwin Arlington Robinson (quoted in *Yesterday and Today* and *This Singing World*). The great majority of villanelles are content to rely on a lightness of execution and the bright ripple of rhyme. The form lends itself to a combination of quaintness and flippancy—as may be observed in this dexterous recent witticism by Franklin P. Adams:

Villanelle, with Stevenson's Assistance

The world is so full of a number of things
    Like music and pictures and statues and plays,
I'm sure we should all be as happy as kings.

We've winters and summers and autumns and springs,
    We've Aprils and Augusts, Octobers and Mays—
The world is so full of a number of things.

Though minor the key of my lyrical strings,
    I change it to major when paeaning praise:
I'm sure we should all be as happy as kings.

Each morning a myriad miracles brings,
    Each evening a myriad marvels conveys,
The world is *so* full of a number of things.

With pansies and roses and pendants and wings,
    With purples and yellows and scarlets and grays,
I'm sure we should all be as happy as kings.

So pardon a bard if he carelessly sings
    A solo indorsing these Beautiful Days—
The world is so full of a number of things,
I'm sure we should all be as happy as kings.

              —Franklin P. Adams

A BRIEF OUTLINE OF ENGLISH POETRY

By Louis Untermeyer and Winifred Howell Davies

FOREWORD

That "familiarity breeds contempt" is, like most proverbs, only occasionally true. In the matter of art, it is wholly false. The more familiar one becomes with a work of art, the more one enjoys it; and appreciation usually follows in exact proportion to understanding. This is not meant to imply that a person will enjoy a particular poem merely because he has heard it continually quoted, but rather that he will enjoy all poems more if he understands something of the craft of poetry and its development through the centuries. The literature of any period is enriched by its backgrounds; the most experimental modern writing acquires a new set of values when one perceives its distant origins. It is fascinating to trace the various tendencies in recent poetry back to the didactic homilies of the Middle Ages, to the almost mathematically precise couplets of Pope, even to the sentimental lyrics of the lesser Victorians, and to note how all these were caught in the swing of convention and revolt, how greatly they were applauded at one time and frowned on at another.

Therefore it is fitting that in a book of this type—a handbook of verse—there should be included some sort of history of the poetry written in the English language. The field is so large that libraries might be devoted to it, and yet even the briefest outline, such as this, may foster a fuller enjoyment of poetry.

Every nation seems to have brought some particular

art to its highest state of development. In general, the German-speaking countries are identified with music, the Dutch and the Italians have never been surpassed as painters, and (possibly because of the very flexibility of the language) the writers of English have expressed the greatest variety of poetry since the Christian era. Philologists have attempted to explain this by the rich mixture of tongues which have formed our speech—the combination of the masculine vigor of the Teutonic roots and the feminine grace of the Latin derivatives. Whatever the explanation, the range as well as the lyrical preëminence of English (and American) poetry must be evident to the most casual reader.

In a history of this sort, any attempt to name *all* the interesting poets would be futile. One can only point to the high lights of each age. Even less can be detailed concerning the poems; only in rare cases is the story of a poem told. Any interested reader should have no difficulty in exploring the originals for himself.

One method by which this history was curtailed—possibly a questionable condensation—was the omission of practically all mention of dramatic literature. But the story of the development of the poetic drama from Shakespeare to Stephen Phillips could more easily be made to fill a quarto volume than be compassed in a cursory chapter. It is with the development of poetry *per se* that this rapid sketch concerns itself.

ANGLO-SAXON POETRY

VII to XI Centuries

The earliest poems which may be claimed as belonging to English literature were not written in English as we know it, but in Anglo-Saxon. The oldest specimens which now exist are found in the Exeter Book, which was given to the library of Exeter cathedral by Leofric, first bishop of Exeter, in the latter half of the Eleventh Century, and in the Vercelli Book, so called because it was found in the Vercelli cathedral in Italy. Among the poems these contain are *Widsith* (or *The Far-Wanderer*), which, though not of great literary value, is interesting on account of the pictures it gives us of a wandering minstrel in early England; *Doer's Lament*, the story of a typical court-poet told with emotional vigor; *The Wanderer* and *The Sea-Farer*, both of these being as full of love of the sea as John Masefield's ballads or the novels of Conrad.

By far the most important poem of this period, however, is the epic of *Beowulf*. It was composed by an unknown poet or poets—probably in the Seventh Century, but the earliest manuscript of it which we possess dates from the Tenth Century and is now in the British Museum. Even to-day it is a thrilling narrative. The story recounts the adventures of Beowulf, a heroic leader, while freeing Denmark from the scourge of Grendel and Grendel's mother, fabulous monsters somewhat akin to the dragons so often encountered in the Scandinavian sagas. The poem consists of more than three thousand lines full of vividly projected adventures.

Not only does the language differ vastly from modern English, but the poetry itself makes use of devices which are quite unlike those employed by later poets. For example, Anglo-Saxon verse does not use rhyme, but is written in alliterative meter. (For a definition of "alliteration," see the section, "A Handbook of Poetic Terms.") When a modern poet writes, he uses alliteration as an added ornament; but the Anglo-Saxon poet delighted in using this artifice throughout his poem.

Each line of *Beowulf* has at least two words which al-
literate, and every line contains one strongly marked
caesura. (See "A Handbook of Poetic Terms" for the
word *caesura*.) Another characteristic of poetry of this
early period is the use of "kennings" (see "A Handbook of Poetic Terms"). These ancient poets, moreover, were fond of making understatements; instead of
saying "the king was angry" they would say "the
king was not very well pleased." This manner of speaking is employed even to-day, but now it is given an
ironic rather than a poetic inflection.

This period also yields a number of other poems by
Christian rather than by pagan poets, poems which were
preserved in the monasteries. The most famous of these
are by Cædmon (the story of whose inspiration to write
was first told by the Venerable Bede in his history of the
church and has since been retold in practically every history of literature) and by Cynewulf. Their material is
chiefly biblical, but their style and characteristics do not
differ from the Anglo-Saxon poems already mentioned.

MEDIEVAL ROMANCES

XI to XIV Centuries

When William the Norman conquered England in
1066, it is probable that he thought of every other form of
victory but the triumph of a literary revolution. Yet the
result of his conquest was felt more keenly in literature
than in any other field. The language underwent an
enormous change as the result of French influence, and so,
too, did literary taste. If the poet who lived about 1100
wished to gain an audience, he was practically compelled
to write what is known as a *metrical romance*. As the
name implies, these poems (usually quite long) were ro-

mantic and dealt with chivalrous adventures, more often than not with a touch of the supernatural in them. They were written chiefly for the edification of the nobility, though no doubt the common people, who had none too much romance in their daily struggles, also enjoyed improbable tales of brave knights rescuing beautiful ladies from pleasantly thrilling dangers.

Most of these romances were written about French legends and many of them were not English at all, but merely translations from the French. However, a few do exist which are specifically English, the most important being *The Gest of King Horn* (the oldest), *Havelok the Dane*, and *Bevis of Hampton*.

One of the most charming and undoubtedly the most enduring of these romances is *Sir Gawain and the Green Knight*, written by an unknown poet. The story is ingratiatingly told, with alert descriptions and keen characterization. (It has been translated into modern English prose and can be read in *Century Readings for a Course in English Literature*, edited by Cunliffe, Pyre, and Young.)

Often a number of romances revolved about a particular event or some prominent person, and when these were gathered into groups they were known as *cycles*. The most famous of these cycles in English literature centers about the story of King Arthur and his knights of the Round Table, one of the earliest English poems in which Arthur is mentioned being the *Brut* (circa 1250), a history of Britain supposedly written by a monk named Layamon. The *Brut* (as well as other romances of this period) makes use of rhyme as well as of alliteration, a significant departure establishing the French influence.

Didactic verse made its appearance about this time; one encounters sermons, called homilies, written in metrical form, probably with the desire to disguise their inherent dullness.

Another type of poem which was in great favor during the Middle Ages was the *bestiary*. Bestiaries (sometimes called by their French name, *fabliaux*) were poems written about animals and birds endowed with human vices and virtues. The material which centers around Reynard the Fox was frequently used as a subject by poets of this age in France and Germany as well as in England. (John Masefield's *Reynard the Fox, or The Ghost Heath Run* (1919) is the best contemporary adaptation of the ancient favorite.) Though their popularity was perhaps more pronounced during this period than at any other time in the history of literature, animal stories as a type have existed—and persisted—in the writings of all countries and in all ages. In India they were a feature of the *Jatakas* and most of them were composed about 400 B.C. A certain slave in Greece entertained his captors with little stories that were much like the Middle English bestiaries, and even to-day his tales are known to most school children as *Aesop's Fables*.

About 1200 some one whose name has been lost to us wrote a long poem of nearly eighteen hundred lines, called *The Owl and the Nightingale*. It is one of the best of the allegorical works, the owl representing duty, and the nightingale, beauty. Their debate concerning the relative importance of the two virtues is interesting, and though the moralizing is obvious, it retains something of the charm it must have had for its original readers.

During these early centuries, hymns came into favor, and it is curious to note that some of them are still sung in our churches. Most of us are familiar with " Jerusalem the Golden," which was written as early as 1150.

Englishmen have always loved Nature (possibly, according to a contemporary, because they see so little of it) and one at least of their earliest Nature poems has come down to us. It begins quaintly thus:

> Sumer is icumen in,
>   Lhude [1] sing cucu!
> Groweth sed,[2] and bloweth med,[3]
>   And springeth the wude nu,
>   Sing, cucu!

CHAUCER AND HIS CONTEMPORARIES

XIV and XV Centuries

GEOFFREY CHAUCER (1340–1400) is often called "the father of English poetry"—a fitting title, for his is the first poet's name to stand out with particular prominence. If one had to choose the four most important poets in all English literature, his would surely be joined with the names of Shakespeare and Milton, though there would probably be a wide difference of opinion regarding the fourth.

Chaucer was the son of a London wine merchant, and, like most boys of the well-to-do class in his day, received his education by serving as a page. When he was nineteen years old, he bore arms in France and was taken prisoner. The king, Edward III, however, ransomed him and later he was sent to the Continent on diplomatic missions. Chaucer went to Italy at least twice—a rare literary privilege, for the Italian Renaissance was then at its height. Dante had died a little earlier, but Petrarch and Boccaccio were writing at this time; and had Chaucer not become acquainted with Boccaccio's *Decameron* (1350) he might never have produced his own related masterpiece, *The Canterbury Tales*.

The Canterbury Tales are stories supposed to be nar-

[1] lhude = loud.   [2] sed = seed.   [3] med = meadow.

rated by a company of pilgrims while on their way to the shrine of St. Thomas à Becket at Canterbury. Chaucer, loving humanity in all its contradictory manifestations, describes with keen sympathy, delightful humor, and good-natured satire each member of the party, and modern readers are frequently more enchanted by these pungent descriptions than by the tales themselves. Among the thirty pilgrims are a Knight, a Prioress, a Clerk, a Wife of Bath, a Monk, a Miller, etc., and their stories are almost as varied as their occupations. The *Tales* are unfinished, as each pilgrim was expected to tell two and Chaucer lived to write only twenty-four of them—and not all of these are complete. He drew upon many sources for his material and it is the way in which he used his material rather than any originality in plot which makes this volume the golden treasury it is. Using rhyme, a definite meter, and alliteration, Chaucer wrote the tales in heroic verse or pentameter (see "The Forms of Poetry"). Even more important was his effect on the language itself. There were a great many dialects in England at this time, and, by showing what rich use could be made of the flexible Midland dialect, Chaucer established it for all time as the literary language of England.

Chaucer was the first to achieve the honor of being buried in the famous "Poets' Corner" in Westminster Abbey. In one of his sonnets, Longfellow wrote of him:

> He is the poet of the dawn, who wrote
> > *The Canterbury Tales*, and his old age
> > Made beautiful with song; and as I read
> I hear the crowing cock, I hear the note
> > Of lark and linnet, and from every page
> > Rise odors of ploughed field or flowery mead.

The best-known poet contemporary with Chaucer is WILLIAM LANGLAND (1332–1400), whose fame rests on

The Vision of Piers Plowman, a long allegorical poem, written in the hope of bringing about a reformation in some of the then existent evils in England, particularly in regard to the oppression of the poor. One of the earliest "poets of protest," he did not advocate a social revolution but a spiritual reform. Langland wrote in the old Anglo-Saxon measure, and this is the last important poem in which it was used.

The Fifteenth Century

During the Fourteenth and Fifteenth Centuries, ballads became suddenly popular, and many of those which have retained their hold on readers to-day—*Lord Randal, Glasgerion,* and the series which has Robin Hood and his "merrie men" for its heroes—were composed at this time. (A brief history of the ballad is given in "The Forms of Poetry.")

JOHN SKELTON (1460–1529) is the principal poet of this period. He was educated at Cambridge and at Oxford, and ranked among the most learned men of his day. Tutor to the prince who later became Henry VIII, Skelton wrote a number of poems, his two richest being *The Boke of Phylyp Sparowe* (written to entertain a young girl grieving over the death of her pet bird) and *Colin Clout,* a rough satire against the corruptions of the Church. He wrote in a rugged, uneven meter—he himself describes his rhymes as "ragged, tattered and jagged"—and his verses, witty and effervescent, were imitated so often that his structure became known as "Skeltonic meter."

Chaucer's poetry received the popularity it deserved and, like all things greatly admired, was widely imitated. The most eminent of Chaucer's direct followers was JAMES I, King of Scotland (1395–1437). *The King's Quair* (1423), a love poem addressed to the niece of England's king, contains many lines which, far from regal, are charming in their tender simplicity. The royal poet made excellent use of (though he did not originate) the seven-line stanza, and because of his employment of the form it has since been called "rime royal." (See "Handbook of Poetic Terms.")

Other Scottish writers—in particular ROBERT HENRYSON (dates uncertain), WILLIAM DUNBAR (1460–1513) and GAVIN DOUGLAS (1474?–1522)—attained no little distinction in a poetry which showed Chaucer's influence to a marked degree. In addition to his original work, Douglas is memorable for his translation of the *Aeneid*, the first complete rendering of an ancient classic into English.

It was toward the end of this century, in 1476 to be exact, that WILLIAM CAXTON returned from Holland and set up at Winchester the first printing-press England had ever had, giving an incalculable impetus to the spread and popularizing of literature.

The Sixteenth Century

In 1557 appeared one of the most interesting books in all English literature. It was entitled *Tottel's Miscellany* and was the first important anthology of English poetry. Finding instant favor, it was soon followed by other collections bearing such intriguing names as *England's Helicon* and *Paradise of Daintie Devices*. This *Miscellany* is also notable for containing the writings of SIR THOMAS WYATT and HENRY HOWARD, Earl of Surrey. Both were important innovators in their day, for Wyatt (1503–1542) was the first to employ the Italian sonnet form in English poetry, and the Earl of Surrey (1517–1547), his younger friend, was the first to introduce blank verse by translating two books of the *Aeneid* into iambic pentameter.

In the latter half of this century lived two other writers whose work entitles them to rank among the greatest of English poets. The first was SIR PHILIP SIDNEY (1554–1586), whose sonnet sequence *Astrophel to Stella* was an outstanding composition of the period and has historical value since it shows the assimilation of the Italian verse form into English poetry, Wyatt's work being more or less experimental. The second was EDMUND SPENSER (1552–1599), whose chief work was *The Faerie Queen*.

Sir Philip Sidney's best known book is his pastoral romance, *Arcadia*, which he wrote to entertain his sister, the Countess of Pembroke, but the major part of it is written in prose with but a few poems interspersed. His sonnets, already mentioned, are imitative of Petrarch's sonnets to Laura, but they possess a charm distinctly their own. There are one hundred and twenty of them, "a metrical necklace" presented to "Stella," a fictitious name for Penelope Devereux, who had married before Sidney met her.

Of Edmund Spenser, John W. Cousin writes: "The position of Spenser in English poetry is below Chaucer, Shakespeare and Milton only. The first far excels him in narrative and constructive power and in humor; but for richness and beauty of imagination and exquisite sweetness of music he is unsurpassed except by Shakespeare." *The Faerie Queen* (the first three books appeared in 1590) is an allegory, written to signify twelve moral virtues; an entire book was to be devoted to each, but only six books were completed. These center about the knights of Holiness, Temperance, Chastity, Friendship, Justice, and Courtesy. Gloriana, the queen of the fairies, represents Queen Elizabeth—a compliment which the noble patroness of literature appreciated. The allegorical story grows rather involved, as nearly every character represents two or three different things, but the whole is typical of the ornate Elizabethan period, with its exaggerated chivalry, its love of fantastic adventure; and it required the richness of Spenser's imagination to give these lavish qualities any vital expression. The stanza form which Spenser used consisted of nine lines (see "The Forms of Poetry") and was widely imitated by other poets.

Spenser's other writings include *The Shepherd's Calendar* (1579), his first important composition, which he dedicated to his dear friend, Sidney. This is a pastoral eclogue, made up of twelve poems, one for each month of the year, dealing with a great variety of subjects. It shows Spenser's interest in Vergil and other Latin classics which so influenced Elizabethan England. His two great lyrical poems, the "Epithalamion" and the "Prothalamion," are like a duet of flutes and little bells, and his series of sonnets, the *Amoretti*, are almost as memorable as Sidney's.

Another important figure of this period is SIR WALTER RALEIGH. Raleigh was the Elizabethan age summed up in one man: he was a courtier, explorer, politician, historian, and poet. His accomplishments in the last rôle are not great in number or quality; his poetical offering, though slight in bulk, is winning, gracefully artificial, and altogether typical of his gallant period.

SHAKESPEARE AND THE GOLDEN AGE OF DRAMA

If it is true that our love of fiction is a desire to participate in a story, how much more do we enjoy watching the action personified and taking place before our eyes. This desire to project ourselves, to identify our own struggles with the triumphs of others or to win a catharsis from their defeats, began with the very infancy of the race. It is implicit not only in the Greek tragedies and the religious ceremonies, but in the primitive rituals of the American Indian and the Congo savages.

Drama began particularly early in the history of the English race. It had its origins in the Church and by the time Queen Elizabeth came to the throne (1558), drama had reached a high pinnacle in its development. *Ralph Roister Doister*, by Nicholas Udall (written before 1550 but printed in 1566), is considered the first definitely English comedy, and the first English tragedy appears to be *Gorboduc*, by Norton and Sackville, which was performed for Queen Elizabeth in 1562. The early miracle and mystery plays, the moralities (of which *Everyman* is the most famous), the masques, and the interludes would make a separate and involved subject for investigation.

In 1587, when Elizabeth had been reigning for over twenty-five years, the "hit" of the theatrical season in London was a roaring, romantic tragedy entitled *Tamburlaine*. Its author was a young man of twenty-three by the name of CHRISTOPHER MARLOWE (1564–1593). He and William Shakespeare were born in the same year (1564), but though Shakespeare was fifty-two years old when he died, Marlowe never reached his thirtieth birthday, for he was killed in a tavern brawl. When Shakespeare was twenty-nine years old he had nine plays to his credit—none of which, however, take their rank among his greatest works. Marlowe's entire reputation rests on the plays—six in number—which he had written up to this time. It has entertained several worthy commentators to compare the genius of these two men and to wonder whether, *if* Marlowe had lived to be as old as Shakespeare and *if* he had been capable of as great a growth, their names would have been linked as Keats's and Shelley's are. Although the following epigrammatic quatrain is not intended to disparage Marlowe's genius, having been written after reading

Marlowe's crudest production (*Tamburlaine the Great*), its author, William Watson, has expressed in four lines what most commentators have failed to embody in as many pages:

> Your Marlowe's page I close, my Shakespeare's ope.
> How welcome—after gong and cymbal's din—
> The continuity, the long slow slope,
> The vast curves of the gradual violin.

This much at least is indubitable: what little we have of Marlowe reveals him as a poet of the first rank, a verbal musician whose lines vibrate with "purple thunder," ringing with deep-toned organ notes like a majestic fugue by Bach.

But far greater than any of the geniuses who have enriched English literature either before or since his day is WILLIAM SHAKESPEARE (1564–1616). The few recorded facts of his life—his birth at Stratford-on-Avon; his marriage to Ann Hathaway at the age of eighteen; his removal a short time later to London, where he became associated with various theaters in the capacities of coach-boy, actor, and, finally, playwright; his return as property-holder to suburban Stratford—these facts are almost too well known to bear repetition. Nor is this the time (or the place) for an appraisal of his adjective-beggaring qualities. If any one characteristic predominates, it is a universal understanding, an almost cosmic sympathy which makes him ageless. He writes with equal intimacy of men of all ranks, from kings to clowns, from lovers to gravediggers. He makes equally real (and eternally modern) the romantic fourteen-year-old Juliet and the ardent young feminist Portia. His plays—nearly forty—include the lightest comedies, the darkest tragedies, and the most brilliantly panoramic histories that have ever appeared on any stage.

If Shakespeare's premier position as dramatist is undisputed, his importance as a poet is scarcely less. He filled every form—from an orchestral blank verse to the most flutelike lyric—with magic and finality. His sonnets, which number among the greatest in the language, constitute one of the most revealing autobiographical fragments of which we have any record. His songs, which have been set to music a thousand times, are the very breath of ecstasy. When to these are added his embodiments of every passion, every phase of human thought, it becomes plain that Shakespeare did not merely create a literature—he created a world.

The dramatist of this period who ranks next to Shakespeare and Marlowe (even above the latter, according to some critics) is BEN JONSON (1555–1637). His writings include half a dozen plays of a new species—the comedy of manners—pastorals, masques, epigrams, lyrics, odes, prose essays, and even an English grammar. He was, incidentally, the first to be appointed Poet Laureate of England. Although it is probable that Jonson and Shakespeare were close friends, their literary ideals were very different. Jonson was one of the premier English classicists and did not believe that comedy and tragedy should ever be combined in one play. His sentences have neither the grace and splendor of Shakespeare's nor the power of Marlowe's "mighty line"; but his best drama, *Every Man in His Humor* (first acted in 1598), still makes diverting reading, and his delicate little love-song, "To Celia," beginning, "Drink to me only with thine eyes," has been sighed by abstainers and bellowed by tipplers from his day to ours.

This period in English history was preëminently the time of the greatest development of the drama. Among the writers of importance in those days GEORGE CHAP-

MAN (1559–1634) deserves mention, though perhaps not so much for his many plays as for his sonorous translation of Homer's *Iliad* and *Odyssey*, a translation which was to form the inspiration two hundred years later for one of literature's greatest sonnets. (See Keats's sonnet " On First Looking into Chapman's Homer," in " The Forms of Poetry" on page 87.)

Marston, Dekker, Massinger, Heywood, and slightly later those famous collaborators, Beaumont and Fletcher, are important names in the history of the drama, but (except for the lyrics of Fletcher) their contribution to poetry *per se* is not great enough to merit a detailed discussion.

CAVALIERS AND PURITANS

The Seventeenth Century

At the death of Elizabeth, the throne passed from the Tudors to the Stuarts. During the reign of James I (1603–1625) few important poets appeared, but when Charles I assumed power (1625–1649) and Oliver Cromwell was endeavoring to gain control of the government, more names became prominent than in the preceding century. The people of this age were divided into two vastly different groups, their differences including more than political or even religious beliefs. On one side were the Cavaliers, typical gentlemen of the court, light-hearted, high-spirited, gallant, audacious, ready to throw away their lives for a whim of the moment provided only that they might meet death with a grand gesture. The other side was made up of Puritans, restrained, religious, philosophical, grimly serious; instead of the pursuit of happiness, their ideal was a contented stability, an almost frozen serenity. These characteristics can be easily discerned in the poetry produced by the two groups.

The Cavaliers found their happiest poetic expression in gay little sparkling lyrics, many of which are well known to-day. The greatest of them was ROBERT HER-RICK (1691–1674). He was prevented by Charles I with a parish in Devonshire, but there was never anything of the unctuous clergyman about him. Although his life was not spent at court, he was typically Carolinian in spirit. In comparison with his secular poems, his *Noble Numbers or Pious Pieces* are uninspired. His fame rests securely upon the volume of 1200 poems entitled *Hesperides* (published in 1648) which contains such immortal mosaics as "Gather Ye Rosebuds While Ye May," "Corinna's Going a-Maying," and "To Daffodils." The following from his pen not only tells the subject matter of his poems, but typifies in his love of "cleanly wantonness" the preoccupations of the other Cavaliers:

> I sing of brooks, of blossoms, birds and bowers,
> Of April, May, of June, and July flowers;
> I sing of May-poles, hock-carts, wassails, wakes,
> Of bridegrooms, brides, and of their bridal cakes.
> I write of Youth, of Love and have access
> By these, to sing of cleanly wantonness;
> I sing of dews, of rains, and, piece by piece,
> Of balm, of oil, of spice, and ambergris;
> I sing of times trans-shifting; and I write
> How roses first came red, and lilies white;
> I write of groves, of twilights, and I sing
> The court of Mab, and of the Fairy King;
> I write of Hell; I sing, and ever shall,
> Of Heaven, and hope to have it after all.

In structure, he was a disciple of Jonson, thus following the classic rather than the Italian style of writing.

The other noteworthy names in this assemblage are THOMAS CAREW (1589–1639), SIR JOHN SUCKLING (1608–1642) and RICHARD LOVELACE (1618–1658). Carew wrote graceful, melodious lyrics which were much more polished in form and expression than most of the fluent and, often, too facile outpourings of this group. Suckling's famous "Why so pale and wan, fond lover?" exemplifies the gayety and *insouciance* found in all his poems. A large portion of the verse of Lovelace is trivial and carelessly written, yet he occasionally reached the highest peaks when he wrote such lines as:

> I could not love thee, dear, so much,
> Loved I not honor more.

and the proverbial:

> Stone walls do not a prison make,
> Nor iron bars a cage.

The name of JOHN DONNE (1572–1631) is most significant because of the vast influence which he exerted over the writers of his century, in particular over the Puritans. He was a doctor of divinity (at one time the King's chaplain) and his work reflects the continual conflict between the body and the spirit; even his religious poems burn with a sensual, almost a tortured, heat. His lyrics are often crowded with more than they can bear: "The Ecstasy" (which Quiller-Couch has quoted in a poorly abbreviated version in *The Oxford Book of English Verse*) is a superb blend of music and metaphysics; "The Flea" is, in its very monstrous conceit, one of the strangest love poems in any language. Neither before nor since the poetry of Donne has there been so great a mixture of grossness and awe.

The term "metaphysical" was applied by Dr. Samuel Johnson to Donne and his followers who employed fantastic imagery, verbal excesses, and delighted in ingenious structures. Their manner was directly opposed to the grace and romanticism of the Elizabethans. The chief representatives of the school are: GEORGE HERBERT (1593–1632), RICHARD CRASHAW (1612–1650), ABRAHAM COWLEY (1618–1667), HENRY VAUGHAN (1621–1695), HENRY KING, Bishop of London (1592–1669), and ANDREW MARVELL (1621–1678), whose immortality is assured by "A Garden" and that magnificent height of ironic banter, "To His Coy Mistress."

"Holy George Herbert" was totally different in character from that other clergyman-poet, Herrick. His seriousness and religious zeal almost rival Milton's, though the bulk of his work can scarcely be mentioned in the same sentence. Herbert's volume of sacred poems, *The Temple*, includes 169 poems, of which 116 are in different meters. Herbert was sometimes more concerned with the manner than with the matter, and many of his writings are artificial and obscure. Yet he was capable of writing such a spontaneous lyric as "Sweet day, so cool, so calm, so bright." Crashaw's work is extremely uneven, sometimes glowing with genuine emotions, sometimes chilled with artificiality. He began life as an ardent member of the Church of England and ended as an equally ardent Roman Catholic; his *Steps to the Temple* contains both sacred and secular poems. Cowley was the author of many Pindaric odes (see "Handbook of Poetic Terms"); his biblical epic, "The Davideis," according to Andrew Lang, fairly "revelled in metaphysical conceits."

The supreme example of Puritan poet is, of course, JOHN MILTON (1608–1674). When Milton was twenty-one, he wrote the "Ode on the Morning of Christ's Nativity" which remains one of the greatest odes in English literature. That classic pair, "L'Allegro" (The Happy Man) and "Il Penseroso" (The Meditative Man), "Comus," a masque in which he first wrote in blank verse, and "Lycidas," a famous elegy, are Milton's "minor" poems, but they show how fecund was his genius. In addition to a number of unforgettable sonnets and the tragedy *Samson Agonistes* he wrote a vast amount of prose. His masterpiece, *Paradise Lost*, takes undisputed place as the greatest English epic.

Keats, in his own idiom, has summarized this epic as follows: "The Genius of Milton, more particularly in respect to its span in immensity, calculated him by a sort of birthright for such an 'argument' as the 'Paradise Lost': he had an exquisite passion for what is properly, in the sense of ease and pleasure, poetical Luxury; and with that, it appears to me, he would fain have been content, if he could, so doing, have preserved his self-respect and feeling for duty performed. But there was working in him, as it were, the same sort of thing as operates in the great world to the end of a Prophecy's being accomplished. Therefore he devoted himself rather to the ardours and the pleasures of song, solacing himself at intervals with cups of old wine, and those are, with some exceptions, the finest parts of the poem." And Coleridge, in a more rhapsodic strain, concludes: "Is not Milton a sublimer poet than Homer or Virgil? Are not his personages more sublimely clothed, and do you not know that there is not perhaps one page in Milton's *Paradise Lost* in which he has not borrowed his imagery from the Scriptures?"

The chief poet of the Restoration period was JOHN DRYDEN (1631–1700), whose verse brimmed with an extraordinary energy. At this time, English literature was reflecting the influence of French poets, in particular of Boileau (1636–1711), whose *L'Art Poétique* advised incessant polishing of every line and advocated the placing of intellect above emotion. This spirit was preparing the way for the most important figure of the Eighteenth Century— Alexander Pope. Dryden won fame as a dramatist, satirist, and writer of odes and lyrics. His early "heroic" plays are written in rhyme, but his greatest drama, *All for Love*, based on the theme of Antony and Cleopatra, follows Shakespeare's model in so far as it is written in blank verse. Dryden's satires were the keenest which had as yet appeared, and *Absalom and Achitophel* still remains one of the greatest of English political satires. *MacFlecknoe* is a more personal and vindictive satire, which Pope used as a model for his *Dunciad*. It has been said of this: "Dryden's method here is something very near to parody; he applies vocabulary, images and ceremony which arouse epic associations of grandeur to make an enemy helplessly ridiculous." He wrote two religious poems; the first, *Religio Laici*, defends with dignity the Church of England, and the second, *The Hind and the Panther*, is an allegorical vindication of Catholicism. The favorite "Song for St. Cecelia's Day" is a magnificent Pindaric ode, though "Alexander's Feast" is more widely quoted in the anthologies. Dryden's prose *Essay on Dramatick Poesie*, in which he discussed the relative merits of rhyme and blank verse, established his reputation as a critic.

Recently there has been a great revival of interest in the Restoration and Metaphysical poets. Dryden in particular has received the plaudits of many of the intellectuals of this generation. T. S. Eliot, one of the most distinguished of these, has published a pamphlet entitled *Homage to John Dryden*, in which the first essay concludes: "Dryden lacked what his master, Jonson, possessed, a large and unique view of life; he lacked insight, he lacked profundity. But where Dryden fails to satisfy, the Nineteenth Century does not satisfy us, either; and where that century has condemned him, it is itself condemned. In the next revolution of taste it is possible that poets may turn to the study of Dryden. He remains one of those who have set standards for English verse which it is desperate to ignore."

SAMUEL BUTLER (1621–1681), not to be confused with the Nineteenth Century novelist of the same name, though less of a poet than Dryden, wrote one of the wittiest and sharpest satires when he produced *Hudibras*. Its design is based on *Don Quixote* and it satirizes Puritanism in brilliant epigram and skillful couplets.

In 1611, the King James version of the Bible was printed, and it is impossible to estimate the effect its sonorously beautiful English has had on subsequent literature.

POPE AND THE AUGUSTAN AGE

The Eighteenth Century

The first quarter of the Eighteenth Century is often called the age of reason. The poets themselves referred to it as "the Augustan Age," for they tried to model their works on the Latin poets who were writing when Augustus was ruler of Rome. It was, generally speaking, an age of prose.

The poetry of the early part of the period shows an enormous change from that of the preceding centuries—a change rather than an advance. Neilson and Thorndike [1] sum up its characteristics as follows: "Its principles . . . were those of neo-classicism; its aim was the reflection of life as perceived through the reason and under the guidance of the great models of the classics. It accepted life as revealed in the manners and actions of men, rather than in their dreams and aspirations. It was critical, realistic, satirical, rather than idealistic. It sought a clear ex-

---

[1] *A History of English Literature*, by W. A. Neilson and A. H. Thorndike. Quoted by permission of The Macmillan Company, publishers. Copyright, 1920.

pression of definite ideas that should be understood by everyone, rather than the suggestion of ideas that were novel or subtle or individual. It was a literature devoted to the city rather than the country, to society rather than the individual, to the intellect rather than the emotions, to manners rather than to the soul."

The principal exponent was ALEXANDER POPE (1688–1744). He was very precocious—according to his own words, "While yet a child, nor yet a fool to fame, I lisped in numbers, for the numbers came." At the age of seventeen, his *Pastorals* were published, four eclogues which show the influence of Spenser as well as of Vergil. His renown, however, is due to *The Rape of the Lock* (1712), one of the most admirable specimens of mock-heroics in the language; to *The Dunciad* and *The Epistle to Dr. Arbuthnot*, brilliantly scathing satires; to the *Essay on Man*, which is superior to the related *Moral Essays;* and to his far from original though excellently expressed *Essay on Criticism*. Pope also translated Homer's *Iliad* and *Odyssey* into the dexterously matched and clinched couplets which he had made so popular. Not only are many of his phrases frequently encountered, but a number of our familiar proverbs originated as phrases in his lines. "Order is Heaven's first law," "As the twig is bent, the tree's inclined," "Presume not God to scan; the proper study of mankind is man," and possibly the best known of all, "Fools rush in where angels fear to tread"—these are all to be found in the work of this fertile and brilliant prosodist.

A number of the writers whose prose has won them an important place in literature dabbled a little in poetry, sometimes with success. Among these may be grouped JOSEPH ADDISON (1672–1719), whose poem *The Campaign* (celebrating the victory of Blenheim and thus gaining him political advancement) and tragedy *Cato* contain various noteworthy lines. DANIEL DEFOE (1661–1731), of such importance as a forerunner of the later novelists, and JONATHAN SWIFT (1667–1745) also occasionally used verse as their medium of expression. SAMUEL JOHNSON (1709–1784), the great lexicographer, wrote a little poetry, though his greatest contribution to this field was his series of critical essays, *Lives of the Poets*. Johnson's friend and follower, OLIVER GOLDSMITH (1728–1774), composed a number of poems, of which *The Deserted Village* remains the best as well as the most popular.

Other early Eighteenth Century poets were MATTHEW PRIOR (1664–1721), writer of witty *vers de société* (see "Handbook of Poetic Terms"); JOHN GAY (1685–1732), noted particularly for his *The Beggar's Opera* and *Trivia*, a satire on London life; and EDWARD YOUNG (1684–1765), a prolific writer who was possibly Pope's closest imitator.

Toward the middle of the century, a different school of writers began to appear. This school was permeated with the spirit of sentimentalism and found its inspiration in the philosophical essays of Lord Shaftesbury. The first poem of any note in which this tendency is definitely recorded is *The Seasons* by JAMES THOMSON (1700–1748). Ernest Bernbaum (in his introduction to the informative *English Poets of the Eighteenth Century*) says: "*The Seasons* was an innovation, and its novelty lay not so much in the choice of the subject as in the interpretation. Didactic as well as descriptive, it was designed not merely to present realistic pictures but to arouse certain explicitly stated thoughts and feelings."

Among Thomson's followers were MARK AKENSIDE (1721–1770); JOSEPH WARTON (1722–1800) and his brother, THOMAS WARTON (1728–1790); THOMAS GRAY (1716–1771); and WILLIAM COLLINS (1721–1759). These poets repudiated the taste of Pope and his disciples for things mannered, and both in theme and in expression their writings became freer from pretense and artifice. A languorous melancholy droops, willow-like, over their work; such titles as "The Grave," "Night Thoughts," and "Death" predominate. Gray's "Elegy Written in a Country Churchyard" (1751) is the ripest expression of this group and has been ranked with the greatest of meditative lyrics. Collins wrote a number of odes whose reticent sweetness has kept them alive, particularly those beginning "How sleep the brave" and "When Music, heavenly maid, was young."

During the seventeen-sixties, a Genevan Swiss by the name of Jean Jacques Rousseau (1712–1778) published three books which brought about a complete revolution in the current philosophy of education, politics, and literature. His theories quickly filtered through the intellectual groups of England and the Continent, gaining an astonishingly large number of followers. Rousseau advocated a recognition of the importance of the individual, a belief in man's innate goodness and his corruption by society, and a return to nature *via* "the simple life." His doctrines were eagerly accepted by the merging groups of humanists and sentimentalists, and by the end of the Eighteenth Century the influence of Pope was wholly lost in the spread of a new romanticism.

In addition to Rousseau, an influence which strengthened the romantic spirit was the publication, in 1760, of poems attributed to Ossian, supposedly a Gaelic poet of the Third Century. In reality the poems were by JAMES MACPHERSON (1736–1795), who alleged that he discovered the originals in Scotland. The book created a sensation. "Here," according to Bernbaum, "was poetry of the loftiest tone, composed in the unlearned Dark Ages, and answering the highest expectation concerning poetry inspired by Nature only. The benevolent magnanimity of the heroes, the sweet sensibility of the heroines, their harmony with Nature's moods (traits which Macpherson had supplied from his own imagination), were the very traits that won the enthusiasm of the public. The poem in its turn stimulated the sentimentalism which had produced it; and henceforth the new school contended on even terms with the old."

In 1765, Bishop Percy's *Reliques of Ancient English Poetry* appeared. This was an anthology of genuine folk songs and ballads of earlier days, and was to exert a great influence over the poets of the next century, particularly Wordsworth and Coleridge.

Three years later (in 1768), there was published another collection of what purported to be the poetic production of a Sixteenth Century monk by the name of Thomas Rowleie. The poems were in truth brilliant forgeries, written by an extraordinary fifteen-year-old boy, THOMAS CHATTERTON (1752–1770). They display incredible maturity and uncanny erudition, and it is one of the tragedies of literature that their young author was so disheartened by the storm of anger which broke after the discovery of the hoax that he committed suicide at the age of seventeen.

Other poets of the time need occupy us less. WILLIAM COWPER (1731–1818) is remembered not so much by pleasing descriptions of nature in poems like *The Task* as by his galloping humoresque, *John Gilpin*. GEORGE CRABBE (1754–1832), disliking the idealized pictures of country life which were current in contemporary poetry, wrote a number of tales in verse (notably *The Village*) in which he shows the generally drab and pitiful life of the poor.

Scotland's beloved ROBERT BURNS (1759–1796) has been acclaimed one of the greatest of lyric poets. Though he wrote most of his poems in the Lowland Scottish dialect, his work is universal in its power of instant communication. His was a genius of adaptation as well as creation; it is difficult to separate the exquisite melodies originated by Burns from the versions of old songs "improved" by him. Although his lyric range was not vast, his expression of the simple singing line was greatly varied. His gift was equally itself in a hundred love songs as poignant as "O my luve's like a red, red rose"; in tales as rollicking as "Tam o' Shanter"; in pictures of home life as unaffected as "The Cottar's Saturday Night"; in verses immortalizing such lowly things as a mountain daisy, a wounded hare, a cowering field-mouse, a louse seen on a lady's bonnet in church.

JAMES BEATTIE (1735–1803) also exerted an appreciable influence upon his fellow poets of Scotland, although he is now remembered because of a single poem, *The Minstrel.*

The century closed with a mystical dreamer, WILLIAM BLAKE (1757–1827), whose illuminations puzzled his contemporaries and whose later prophetic work continues to baffle most of his readers to-day. Blake was, first of all, a cosmic visionary, "an artist on fire," who illustrated his lines with drawings and engravings as guileless and as terrific as the poetry itself. His undying *Songs of Innocence* are an inspired child's reactions to the common miracles about him; his *Songs of Experience* are no less innocent for all their passionate wisdom. Concerning the linking of Shakespeare and Blake, S. Foster Damon, Blake's most sensitive interpreter, has written the final word. Realizing the absurdity of such a comparison, Damon writes: "Great men can seldom be compared with one another. Nevertheless, the two fit curiously together: Blake was the complement of Shakespeare. The Elizabethan poet recorded all the types of humanity but one—

the mystic: the Georgian recorded no other but the mystic. One saw individuals everywhere; the other saw man. The first hardly systematized human problems; he beheld only situations to whose solution he gave no clue; the second saw problems everywhere, to be solved by reason under the guidance of inspiration. One hid himself, and identified himself so well with his creations that we can hardly say what Shakespeare was like; while from Blake's writings we could reconstruct his very features. Shakespeare found life a dream rounded by the sleep of death: Blake found life a dream to be followed by a more glorious awakening than we can possibly imagine. Both were poets who translated everything into the terms of humanity. . . . Here lies the root of Blake's greatness. His feet stride from mountain to mountain; and if his head is lost among stars and clouds, it is only because he is a giant. His God is not a dim and awful principle; he is a friend who descends and raises man until man is himself a God."

THE NINETEENTH CENTURY

Statistically, at least, the Nineteenth Century contributed more to poetry than any of the preceding centuries. From the Lake poets through the Victorians, the record is strewn with memorable names. In this century, too, the poetry written in America first assumed actual literary value.

The first poem to be written on an American theme (according to Professor Onderdonk in his *History of American Verse*) by a person who had actually lived in this country, was "Newes From America," by one who signed himself "R. Rich, Gent., One of the Voyage." It was printed in London in 1610 and most of it is dull doggerel. *The Bay Psalm Book*, published in 1640, enjoyed considerable prestige in its day, yet it was a shocking and offensive distortion of the beautiful biblical English into the crudest of jingles. An appreciable amount of translating from the classics, but very little original work, appeared in the early days of the States. Among the earliest American poets were ANNE BRADSTREET (1612–1672), MICHAEL WIGGLESWORTH (1631–1705), and PHILIP FRENEAU (1752–1832), whose tiny poetic flames were magnified by their patriotic contemporaries into beacon lights.

A group known as the "Hartford Wits" emerged late in the Eighteenth Century. It included TIMOTHY DWIGHT (752–1817), JOEL BARLOW (1755–1812), and JOHN TRUMBULL (1750–1831). Their work was altogether derivative, most of it being weakly reminiscent of Pope. A little later, the "Knickerbocker School" flourished. JOSEPH RODMAN DRAKE (1795–1820), author of "The American Flag" and "The Culprit Fay," and his close friend, FITZ-GREENE HALLECK (1790–1867), who wrote that favorite of the young elocutionist, "Marco Bozzaris," were the leaders of this school, which also numbered among its members GEORGE P. MORRIS (1802–1864), author of the often quoted "Woodman, Spare That Tree"; SAMUEL WOODWORTH (1785–1842), who has survived by virtue of a single poem, "The Old Oaken Bucket"; and NATHANIEL PARKER WILLIS (1806–1867), a journalist whose light verse is a cheerful contrast to the sentimentalism of the others, but whose serious work is very sad indeed.

The first notable poet born in America (who was sometimes called "The Father of American Poetry") was WILLIAM CULLEN BRYANT (1794–1878). "Thanatopsis" (originally published in 1817), Bryant's first really significant poem, was written at the age of eighteen, though his initial volume of verse, containing eight poems—among them "Thanatopsis" and "To a Waterfowl"—was not published until four years later, in 1821. Bryant's treatment of Nature shows the influence of Wordsworth and, occasionally, a much diluted Shelley. "His range is narrow," concludes the enthusiastic Curtis Hidden Page, "but within his range he is supreme. What he gives us is the expression of simple and noble thoughts on life, and still more on death, and our first expression of American Nature in poetry." On the other hand, Lowell, his friend and contemporary, summarized him as follows:

> There is Bryant, as quiet, as cool, and as dignified,
> As a smooth, silent iceberg, that never has ignified,
> Save when by reflection 'tis kindled o' nights
> With a semblance of flame by the chill Northern Lights.
> He may rank (Griswold says so) first bard of your nation
> (There's no doubt that he stands in supreme ice-olation),
> Your topmost Parnassus he may set his heel on,
> But no warm applauses come, peal following peal on,—
> He's too smooth and too polished to hang any seal on.

After Bryant (chronologically, that is) comes the southern poet, EDGAR ALLAN POE (1809–1849). Poe is one of the few writers who have created noble prose and poetry with equal felicity. His poems number less than fifty and almost all of them are short: "There can be no such thing as a long poem," was one of his several definite rules for the construction of poetry; "what we call a long poem is only a succession of short melodies." Europe appreciated his genius from the first; to-day, whenever American literature is discussed abroad, two names are immediately mentioned: Poe and Whitman. "The fascination of his verse is not due to the depth of thought, to the spiritual penetration of his imagination, or to the poetic setting of noble ideals, for he lacked these qualities. But he was a master in securing emotional effects with his sad music. He wedded his songs of the death of beautiful women to the most wonderful melodies, which at times almost transcend the limits of language and pass into the realm of pure music."

Toward the middle of the century, there appeared the most famous association of American poets: the New England group. This consisted of HENRY WADSWORTH LONGFELLOW (1807–1882), RALPH WALDO EMERSON (1803–1882), JOHN GREENLEAF WHITTER (1807–1892), OLIVER WENDELL HOLMES (1809–1894), and JAMES RUSSELL LOWELL (1819–1891).

No other American poet has enjoyed such widespread popularity as Longfellow. For years he held first place in the affections of his countrymen, and it is only recently that his strong moralizing impulse has caused people to belittle his achievement. One of the qualities which has gained him so large a following is his story-telling faculty. Artistically, perhaps, his sonnets rank higher than his narratives and rhymed sermons, but he is chiefly known and still loved for such tales in verse as *Paul Revere's Ride*, *King Robert of Sicily*, *The Bell of Atri*, and *The Saga of King Olaf*. His is the distinction of having written the nearest approach to a native epic which this country as yet possesses: *Hiawatha* (1857). It was written in trochaic tetrameter (see "Handbook of Poetic Terms"), a meter not newly invented, but rarely used before this time. Longfellow, an ardent delver into foreign languages and literatures, had been much interested in the *Kalevala*, an ancient epic of Finland, and decided to embody his own material in its meter. His two other long narratives, *Evangeline* (1847), written in unrhymed dactylic hexameter, and *The Courtship of Miles Standish* (1858), both dealing with American themes, are equally well known. Longfellow attempted two other works on a grand scale: *Christus, A Mystery* (1872), a trilogy consisting of *The*

Divine Tragedy, The Golden Legend, and *The New England Tragedies;* and *The Tales of a Wayside Inn* (1863), in which he used the framework of *The Canterbury Tales* for his structure. Both of these larger efforts are more successful in their parts than the whole. Longfellow's contribution to the development of literature in this country should not be underrated. By his translations from many European literatures he widened cultural appreciation and, at his best, became a poet of definite distinction.

Ralph Waldo Emerson composed verse which, from the musical standpoint, was far from euphonious. In his writing, the philosopher was always in the ascendant. His was, as Lowell cogently put it, "a Greek head on right Yankee shoulders"; his thoughts, if not always his words, were "gold nails to hang trophies on." Although his poetry was more searching and intellectual than sensuous, Emerson evoked some vivid and even playful descriptions of Nature, one of the best being "The Snowstorm."

Whittier is often referred to as "the antislavery poet," for the larger part of his writings is concerned with the grave question which was then agitating the United States. Though a few of these poems—for example, "Massachusetts to Virginia" and "The Farewell"—contain more than temporary interest, it is under the not unjustified title of "the poet of New England country life" that he is best known and liked. Lacking the universality of Burns, he was, nevertheless, not distantly related to the Scottish bard. Such simple lyrics as "The Huskers," "The Barefoot Boy," and "In School-Days" will probably survive the larger *Snow-Bound.* "A Winter Idyl" contains descriptive lines which, for their straightforward fantasy, have seldom been surpassed in American poetry, and as a writer of hymns, this Quaker poet ranks among the few whose sentiment was not sunk in sentimentality.

Holmes, the most versatile of the group, occupies a position several rungs lower than the others. "The autocrat of the breakfast table" was particularly successful within the limited field of the genial essay, the writing of occasional verse and humorous ballads. In this vein, "The Deacon's Masterpiece" is his *chef d'œuvre*. Equally memorable is "The Last Leaf," written in an unusual meter, with its humor matched by a wry pathos.

Lowell was the equal of Holmes in wit and his superior in many ways. His most famous works are "The Vision of Sir Launfal" and *The Biglow Papers*, a series of political satires written in Yankee dialect; his most delightful record is that remarkable *jeu d'esprit*, *A Fable for Critics*, in which all the leading figures of the day are satirized. Writing of himself (the poem first appeared anonymously), Lowell summarized his characteristics pithily:

There is Lowell, who's striving Parnassus to climb
With a whole bale of *isms* tied together with rhyme;
He might get on alone, spite of brambles and boulders,
But he can't with that bundle he has on his shoulders.
The top of the hill he will ne'er come nigh reaching
Till he learns the distinction 'twixt singing and preaching;
His lyre has some chords that would ring pretty well,
But he'd rather by half make a drum of the shell.

While poetry was germinating, so to speak, in America, it was going through important stages in its development in England.

WILLIAM WORDSWORTH (1770–1850), who followed Rousseau's doctrine of a return to Nature more closely than most, and SAMUEL TAYLOR COLERIDGE (1772–1834), in whose *Ancient Mariner* romantic poetry reached a triumph, together brought out an epoch-making volume, *Lyrical Ballads and Other Poems*, in 1798. This volume not only offered itself as a contribution to poetry *per se*, but served as a protest against the stilted, unnatural diction which was commonly employed by the authors' immediate forerunners. Wordsworth wished to intensify everyday experiences; Coleridge wished to invest the supernatural with an inescapable simplicity.

George Saintsbury has written of Wordsworth: "His real poetical merits are threefold, and lie first in the inexplicable, the ultimate felicity of phrase which all great poets must have, and which only great poets have; secondly, in his matchless power of delineating natural objects; and lastly, more properly, and with most special rarity of all, in the half-pantheistic mysticism which always lies behind this observation and which every now and then breaks through it, puts it, as mere observation, aside, and blazes in unmasked fire of rapture." His sustained "Ode on the Intimations of Immortality" and "Lines Composed a Few Miles Above Tintern Abbey" are the culminating points of his work, though his sonnets and a few magical lyrics have attained permanence.

Coleridge wrote a much smaller amount of poetry, of which *The Rime of the Ancient Mariner* is his masterpiece. *Christabel* and *Kubla Khan* are even more glorious though fragmentary, *Kubla Khan* being one of the most breath-taking pieces of sheer wizardry in the language.

ROBERT SOUTHEY (1774–1843), the close associate of Wordsworth and Coleridge, was the next most important of the "Lake poets," so called because Wordsworth, Coleridge, and Southey spent much of their time in the Lake district of northern England. Although he produced an extraordinary number of poems, the majority of his works are almost unknown to-day and he would have practically no readers were it not for "The Cataract of Lodore."

WALTER SCOTT (1771–1832), less interesting as a poet

than as a novelist, became prominent at the beginning of the new century. His prose established him but his three long poems, *The Lay of the Last Minstrel*, *Marmion*, and *The Lady of the Lake*, contain many often-quoted passages and have achieved at least a classroom popularity. In 1802, he brought out a collection of old ballads and a few of his own, entitled *The Minstrelsy of the Scottish Border*, a book which exerted a decided influence for about a decade.

While still in college, GEORGE GORDON, LORD BYRON (1778–1824), published a little volume of poems, *Hours of Idleness*. This was so harshly treated by the critics that Byron, in wounded pride, wrote *English Bards and Scotch Reviewers*, a bitterly brilliant satire. Subsequently he wrote a number of dramas and short lyrics, but his fame rests chiefly on two long poems, *Childe Harold's Pilgrimage* and *Don Juan*. In the first of these narratives, Childe Harold (a pseudonym for Byron himself) journeys through Portugal, Spain, the Mediterranean Sea, and Greece, soliloquizing in the vein of an inspired guidebook. *Childe Harold* also contains some of Byron's best reflective and pictorial lines as well as the spirit of revolt which manifested itself in whatever Byron wrote. *Don Juan* recounts the amatory adventures of a Spanish libertine in a satirical manner, the numerous episodes being full of a dashing *joie de vivre* in rhymes almost as reckless and one might even say foot-loose as the exploits they celebrate.

For imagination, melody, and sheer beauty of expression, the poems of PERCY BYSSHE SHELLEY (1792–1822) and JOHN KEATS (1795–1821) have never been surpassed. Their names are usually linked, though they possessed nearly as many different characteristics as likenesses. Shelley was a defiant revolutionist, Keats a delighted sensualist; Shelley was "a flame of protest," Keats accepted the world, even when it was most cruel to him.

It has often been charged against Shelley that the ideal which he pursued was not a possible one for the rest of humanity. Himself "a fiery martyr," he foresaw this criticism and in the very preface to *Prometheus Unbound* he wrote: "It is a mistake to suppose that I dedicate my poetical compositions solely to the direct enforcement of reform, or that I consider them in any degree as containing a reasoned system on the theory of human life." In fact, Shelley's poetry offers us no definite program, but as one critic, Walter Raleigh, has recently written: "The very vagueness of Shelley's poetry is an essential part of its charm. He speaks the language of pure emotion, where definite perceptions are melted in the mood they generate. Possessed by the desire of escape, he gazes calmly and steadily on nothing of earthly build. Every visible object is merely another starting-point for the cobwebs of dreams."

His human figures and even his landscapes are ghostly and take on the lyrical indefiniteness

> of some world far from ours,
> Where music and moonlight and feeling are one.

And if Shelley dealt with the abstract passions rather than with more concrete human interests, no one can doubt the leaping strength of his genius. It is always itself and master of itself, whether he writes a "Hymn to Intellectual Beauty," a rebellious psychological portrayal of the Promethean spirit, a sweeping dirge like "Adonais," an "Ode to the West Wind" or "To a Skylark" with its piercing high notes, or lyrics as poignantly sudden as "Music, when soft voices die."

The story of Keats has been written so often that a

reiteration of his struggles against ill-health and critical scorn, even if it were possible to condense it within the limits of this chapter, would be superfluous. Sidney Colvin's biography still stands as the most authoritative résumé and Amy Lowell's crowded two volumes form an even more detailed interpretation. Surpassing all his other qualities there is, as any reader will perceive at once, a heightening and almost conscious intensification of feeling. In contrast to the intellectual element in Shelley, Keats wrote, "O for a life of sensations rather than thoughts!" This hypersensuousness is apparent in practically every line he wrote, in the rich and over-burdened *Endymion* as well as in the luxuriant sonnets; in the purposely antique "La Belle Dame sans Merci," as well as in the lush odes; in that multicolored tapestry, "The Eve of St. Agnes," and the light-diffusing verses beginning "I stood tiptoe upon a little hill." His death at the age of twenty-five (immortalized by Shelley in his lament "Adonais") has given rise to much speculation whether Keats died at the height of his power or at the beginning of a new phase in his creative life. Conrad Aiken, in a brilliantly concise study, claims that "Keats, greatly influenced by Chatterton not only in his work but also in his life, was almost warped by a death-ob-session." "Love, fame and death," concludes Aiken, "were Keats' three graces. The death of a young poet was almost the most tragic (and attractive!) thing he could imagine. The death of a young poet while in love, however, was a turn of the screw which, if he had con-ceived, he had certainly not discounted. When he realized that this was to be his destiny, his imagination gave it fullest value and he died, as passionately and uncon-trolledly and *consciously* as he had lived. He grasped death with all his senses and went under the earth alive."

Lesser poets of this era were THOMAS MOORE (1779–1852), who enriched poetical literature with his charming Irish melodies and the fanciful oriental tale, *Lalla Rookh* (1817); THOMAS HOOD (1799–1845), whose "Bridge of Sighs" and "Song of the Shirt" stand out as the two serious poems in a mass of adroit humorous verse; JAMES HOGG (1772–1835), who helped Scott collect his Border ballads and later wrote a volume of imitative ballads entitled *The Mountain Bard;* WALTER SAVAGE LANDOR (1775–1864), whose poetry, though never granted as high a place as his prose, is cameo-like in its small precisions; THOMAS BABINGTON MACAULAY (1800–1859), whose *Lays of Ancient Rome* were popular rhymed narratives; and COVENTRY PATMORE (1823–1896), who sounded what might be called a domesticated metaphysical note in *The Angel in the House.*

ROBERT BROWNING (1812–1889), "the Shakespeare of the Nineteenth Century," suffered for a time because of the very strength of his idiom. To-day it is conceded that no more many-sided, continually stimulating poet ever existed. His was a mind in which poetry and intellect were beautifully balanced, and, though the ear is often displeased by what seems to be a verbal carelessness or tone-deafness on the part of the craftsman, the intellect is always roused and the heart invariably stirred. Although his fragmentary *Pauline* was published when he was only twenty-one, fame did not reach him until he was past forty. *Men and Women* (1855) is a collection which reflects the variety and vicissitudes of the soul. "Nothing else," wrote Browning, "is worth study." But it is not a disembodied spirit which preoccupies this poet; it is a mingling of "finite clod" and "a God though in the germ" which is celebrated by his own Rabbi Ben Ezra:

Nor soul helps flesh more now than flesh helps soul.

As he grew older, Browning's work became progressively philosophical, and his characters, less sharply delineated, became more the projections of the poet's opinions. Many critics have found fault with his "incorrigible optimism." But it is these critics, rather than Browning, who have overstressed the note of "God's in His Heaven, all's right with the world." Browning's own philosophy is never that of complacent submission. When he accepts, it is because he has won through the shock of struggle; his ringing "yea" is no glib affirmative but a brave reply, challenging and even welcoming "life's rebuffs." Apart from his panoramic romances and suggestive monologues, his work is liberally strewn with some of the most dramatic lyrics in the language. "Had Browning lived in the age of Shakespeare," says Richard Garnett, "he would have been the second greatest English dramatist." His range alone is stupendous; he continues to delight children as well as metaphysicians. Beginning at the age of eight with "The Pied Piper of Hamelin" and ending at eighty with *The Ring and the Book*, a person might well go through life accompanied by no other writer.

Elizabeth Barrett Browning (1806–1861) is the first woman poet to achieve what seems to be a lasting place in English literature. Although she had written poetry since her girlhood, it was not until after her marriage in 1846 to Robert Browning, who was six years her junior, that she wrote the verses with which she is identified to-day. Her greatest effort, a sequence of love poems which she called *Sonnets from the Portuguese* (1850), is an immortal tribute to her poet-husband. Four years later, *Aurora Leigh*, a novel in blank verse, appeared and increased the number of her readers.

At this time another woman poet was beginning to publish her reticent verses. Less popular than Mrs.

Browning, CHRISTINA GEORGINA ROSSETTI (1830–1894) composed a far more intensified poetry, and her religious as well as her definitely personal exaltations are the very outcries of a passionately stirred spirit. Her sonnets are among the purest of their kind, and Swinburne, writing of one of her devotional poems ("Passing Away"), exclaimed: "It is so much the noblest sacred poem in our language that there is none which comes near it enough to stand second." She was the sister of the artist and poet, DANTE GABRIEL ROSSETTI (1828–1882), remarkable not only for his luminous canvases but for the sonnet sequence, *The House of Life*, and "The Blessed Damozel," in which the influence of Keats is obvious.

Both the Rossettis belonged to the group known as the Pre-Raphaelite Brotherhood, a group composed of such painters as Burne-Jones, Ford Madox Brown, William Holman Hunt, John Everett Millais, and such literary persons as the Rossettis, William Morris, and A. C. Swinburne. The Pre-Raphaelites, endeavoring to capture the spirit of Botticelli, Fra Angelico, and the other early Italian painters, brought a romantic mysticism and a curiously sophisticated simplicity to the literature of the period.

THE VICTORIAN ERA

The period known as the Victorian Age presented a large variety of effort in many forms and fields, although the general philosophy of the times seems to have been one of "sweetness and light." It was an age distinguished by many true idealists and many false ideals. It was, in spite of its leaders, on an entirely different plane from the epoch which had preceded it. The poets of the generation before were fired with the principles of liberty, an almost revolutionary freedom, with a passionate intimacy with nature, with a burning hunger for truth in a world of illimitable perplexities. The Victorian era was not universal but parochial; its romanticism was red plush and tinsel; most of its authors, according to Max Plowman, "wrote under the dominance of sanctimoniousness, of the proverbial 'sweetness and light' and a thousand lesser theories and had not truth but comfort for their end." At its worst, it was a period of smugness, of complacent sentimentality, epitomized by the rhymed sermons of Martin Farquhar Tupper, whose *Proverbial Philosophy* was devoured by tens of thousands. At its best, it rose to certain emotional heights in Alfred Lord Tennyson and the philosophic austerities of Matthew Arnold.

The Pre-Raphaelites represented another "escape from reality." Theirs was a movement toward an esthetic freedom (later Oscar Wilde was to use this very estheticism as a slogan) and its chief figures were wholly out of sympathy with their times. Of the Pre-Raphaelite poets, the two Rossettis have already been discussed.

The most outstanding poet of this group was A. C. Swinburne (1837-1909). Although his antecedents were those of the aristocracy (he was the grandson of an earl), Swinburne became notorious for his revolutionary utterances, and it was these very violences which kept him from being named Poet Laureate after the death of Tennyson. His *Poems and Ballads* (sometimes published under the title *Laus Veneris*) caused a sensation and was considered a masterpiece of erotic literature. These verses and the succeeding series proved him an expert in metrical ingenuity and in the phonetics of the language. Writing in every known measure of English verse, Swinburne even invented some of his own. He surpassed all the other practitioners of the French forms and created a new one, the roundel—of which he composed a hundred examples (see "Handbook of Poetic Terms"). His very stress on the musical element in poetry and his extraordinary verbal ease were his greatest weaknesses; the reader is so often rocked by the swing of his lines and lulled by the continual alliteration that he is scarcely conscious of what the poet is trying to say. The poetry of Swinburne is—if a change in metaphor is allowed—like a sparkling but heavy sea in which the reader sinks beneath rhythmical waves and the surge of beautiful syllables.

Although his contribution to poetry was far less important, WILLIAM MORRIS (1834–1896), more than most of his generation, helped to change the public taste in color and design. He not only was devoted to literature but studied painting, turned his attention to architecture, and was a manufacturer of art fabrics, wall papers, stained glass, and books. As a writer, he was eminent not only for his many translations and a rendering of the Anglo-Saxon epic *Beowulf*, but for *The Earthly Paradise* (1868–1870), a series of twenty-four tales modeled roughly after Chaucer. His medievalism was more genuine than most and the narratives themselves display a high quality of imagination.

ALFRED TENNYSON (1809–1892)—he was raised to the peerage and became Lord Tennyson in 1874—was the most representative poet of the Victorian spirit. His work achieved a popularity such as few poets have lived to enjoy. The reasons for Tennyson's great following are twofold: he appealed to the artisan because of his technical skill and excellence of construction, and he found favor with those not ordinarily fond of poetry because of his ability to project tales and dramas in an unusually readable verse. His range, though not nearly so great as Browning's, was extraordinarily wide. His gamut included lyrics as haunting as those in the sentimental romance *Maud;* reflections of a panoramic though somewhat prettified medievalism, as in the epical *Idylls of the King* (1859); such favorites of the elocutionist as "The Charge of the Light Brigade," and the famous elegy *In Memoriam,* in which Tennyson rose to his greatest heights. Whether he wrote a Victorian version of the domestic triangle in *Enoch Arden,* dialect interpretations of *The Northern Farmer,* or historical dramas like *Queen Mary* and the later *Becket* (1884), he revealed not merely a broad cultural background but a keen concern with the problems of his day. Herbert J. Grierson, in the *Cambridge History of English Literature,* has written of him: "An imagination rich in color, a delicate and highly trained ear, a thought which if not profound was nourished on the literature and philosophy of Greece and Rome—these were among Tennyson's gifts to English poetry. . . . He was a great sensitive soul, full of British prejudices but also with a British conscience, anxious to render a good account of the talent entrusted to him, to make art the handmaid of duty and faith."

Among the somewhat less famous Victorians a high place must be given to MATTHEW ARNOLD (1822–1888), chiefly known as a provocative critic and essayist, who wrote comparatively little poetry. In spirit he was more akin to Browning than to Tennyson. Although he found his greatest impetus in the Greek poets, his writing is tinged with the Wordsworthian idiom. *Sohrab and Rustum,* Homeric in style, written in a skillful blank verse, is possibly his best-known poem, though "Dover Beach" attains far greater heights. Arnold's outstanding characteristics are a pensive melancholy and a tendency (in common with others of his age) to emphasize the "moral aspect" of life.

EDWARD FITZGERALD (1809–1883) retains his hold on

the memory as well as the affection of his readers because of his masterly adaptation of *The Rubáiyát of Omar Khayyám.* First published in 1859, it was a pronounced contribution to if not an influence upon the thought of the times. Its philosophy was careless and even definitely pessimistic (a sort of reckless *carpe diem*), but it was framed in a verse so charming and a phrasing so felicitous that it became and remains one of the most popular books of the last seventy-five years.

Other characteristic poets of the period were WILFRID SCAWEN BLUNT (1840–1922), whose remarkable *My Diaries*, appearing when the author was an octogenarian, revealed him as a stout fighter against diplomatic hypocrisy, and whose *Love Sonnets of Proteus* (1871) were more widely read than most sequences; GEORGE MEREDITH (1828–1909), renowned as a novelist and remembered as a poet chiefly because of his "The Woods of Westermain" and "Love in the Valley"; ARTHUR HUGH CLOUGH (1819–1861), whose life and death inspired Arnold's "The Scholar Gipsy"; and JAMES THOMSON (1834–1882), known as "the prophet of despair," and noted for his Dürer-like series of monologues, *The City of Dreadful Night*.

Humorous verse of a sparkling vivacity was written in the late Nineteenth Century by such immortals as W. S. GILBERT, author of the collection of ruthless rhymes, *The Bab Ballads*, and collaborator of Arthur Sullivan in the equally diverting light operas, *Pinafore*, *Patience*, *The Mikado*, etc., which are as dear to their audiences to-day as they were two generations ago; EDWARD LEAR, author of the *Book of Nonsense* and creator of the limerick; FREDERICK LOCKER-LAMPSON, CHARLES STUART CALVERLEY, and LEWIS CARROLL, who incorporated some of the most delightful nonsense verse ever imagined in his perennially enchanting *Alice* books.

POETRY OF OUR DAY: "ROMANTIC REALISM"

England

The era commonly called Victorian came to an end about 1890. Before literary England had recovered from its surfeit of tea-table moralizing and Pre-Raphaelite delicacy, RUDYARD KIPLING (1865–) came out of India with high spirits and a great tide of life, sweeping all before him. As a writer of short stories and tales for children he had few equals; considered solely as a poet, Kipling was one of the most vigorous and certain figures of his time. The spirit of romance surged under his realities; his poetry was woven of the very stuff of myths, but it never lost its hold on actualities. His several volumes of poems (among them the infectious *Departmental Ditties* and *Barrack-Room Ballads*) were collected into a remarkable one-volume *Inclusive Edition* (*1885–1918*). Kipling attracted many imitators on both sides of the Atlantic, chiefly because of his pronounced rhythmical stress, his lines marching along with insistent drumbeats, augmented by frequent interior rhymes, and his unflagging gusto.

What drew the average reader to Kipling was not only the high spirits and loose swing of his lines but his attitude to the world's work. Where others of his day were celebrating limp lilies and languid leisures, Kipling chanted the difficulties of toil; where others were resuscitating mythological legends, Kipling glorified bridge-builders, engineers, stokers, and all those battling in the front ranks of labor.

WILLIAM ERNEST HENLEY (1849–1903) was another who repudiated the loose estheticism which under the banner of Wilde had become a vogue. Henley's was a large and sweeping affirmation. Life to him was coarse, difficult, often dangerous and dirty, but splendid at the heart.

Art, he felt, could not be separated from the aims and hungers of man; to establish the closest contacts, poetry must share the dreams and struggles of a prosaic world. Though Henley's poetry was often overmuscular and almost blatantly imperialistic, his personal enthusiasms were marked by a vigor that is often as straightforward as the ringing "Invictus" in one genre and the simple lyric, "The Blackbird," on the other.

No mention of Henley would be complete without a reference to ROBERT LOUIS STEVENSON (1850–1894), whose essays and novels require no comment. How closely Stevenson's personality was mixed with his writing is evident in all his work, particularly in the two volumes of poems, *Underwoods*, and the modern set of nursery rhymes, *A Child's Garden of Verses*.

Shortly before this time a group of writers established themselves and in the Eighteen-Nineties devoted themselves to a curious preoccupation with the fine arts which was more of a decadence than a renaissance. "It was," according to Holbrook Jackson's *The Eighteen-Nineties*, "a passing mood which gave the poetry of the hour a hothouse fragrance; a perfume faint, yet unmistakable and strange." Its organ was the magazine, *The Yellow Book* (1894–1897), its artist was Aubrey Beardsley, and its chief protagonist was OSCAR WILDE (1859–1900). Beginning as a brilliant undergraduate, Wilde quickly became known as a writer of flashing epigrammatic essays and even more dazzling paradoxical plays, his aphorisms and flippancies being quoted everywhere. Most of his poems in prose (such as *The Happy Prince*, *The Birthday of the Infanta*, and *The Fisherman and His Soul*) are more imaginative and richly colored than his verse; but in one long poem, *The Ballad of Reading Gaol* (1898), he sounded his deepest, most unaffected, and most enduring note.

Other poets associated with the famous closing decade were ARTHUR SYMONS (1865–   ), RICHARD LE GALLIENNE (1866–   ) and ERNEST DOWSON (1867–1900), two or three of whose lyrics bid fair to outlive most of the poetry of his group.

Shortly before this, WILLIAM BUTLER YEATS (1865–   ) had published his *Wanderings of Oisin*. At the same time Douglas Hyde brought out his *Book of Gaelic Stories*, and the Celtic revival followed. Its aim was to create a literature which would express the national consciousness of Ireland through a purely national art. The leaders of the movement were William Butler Yeats, LADY GREGORY, "A. E." (George W. Russell, 1867–   ), and J. M. SYNGE (1871–1909), who joined the movement in 1903. Other members who have since achieved poetic celebrity are LIONEL JOHNSON (1867–1902), MOIRA O'NEILL, KATHARINE TYNAN (1861–   ), and PADRAIC COLUM (1881–   ). The poetry of Yeats is in striking contrast with that of Synge. Yeats's is a richly musical verse, drenched in a lyricism full of overtones; Synge's is brusque and earth-stained, "as fully flavored as a nut or apple."

Something of this tang of the soil is in the work of THOMAS HARDY (1840–   ), an almost acrid taste which is as pronounced in his verse as in his prose. Hardy was almost sixty years old and had already won international fame as a novelist when he began to challenge attention as a poet. He wrote in almost every meter, old and new, but his closely packed intensity was at its richest in the ballad measures which he preferred and in which his narrative genius was given full play. As a chronicle-poet, Hardy spread an epic upon the largest canvas of his time: *The Dynasts* (which appeared in three parts in 1904-6-8) is a drama of the Napoleonic Wars, a massive structure in three books, nineteen acts, and one hundred and thirty scenes. While its tragic impressiveness overshadows the author's shorter poems, even his tersest lyrics vibrate with something of the same vigor and knotted strength.

In 1893 there appeared a small quarto volume of poems which, neglected by the multitude, caused a sensation among the few who recognized in it the accent of greatness. Its author was an unknown FRANCIS THOMPSON (1857–1907), a poverty-stricken outcast who had been forced to earn his living selling shoes, carrying parcels for a bookseller, and waiting at the doors of theaters to call cabs. Upon the publication of his ode, "The Hound of Heaven," the first of his reviewers (Richard Le Gallienne) wrote: "Francis Thompson must simply be Crashaw born again, but born greater." In subtlety of expression, richness of imagery and daring use of archaic epithets, Thompson established himself as a poet of the first rank. His was an exuberant genius, a "wassail of orgiac imagery," and if his work suffers from "superabundance" it is because his spirit was so lavish that it took no note of economy in speech. G. K. Chesterton, answering the charge of obscurity, summed up his essential quality when he wrote: "Great poets are obscure for two opposite reasons: now, because they are talking about something too large for anyone to understand and now, again, because they are talking about something too small for anyone to see. Francis Thompson possessed both these infinities."

A few years after the publication of Thompson's first volume, a collection of lyrics appeared which by its very simplicity of utterance was to influence an entire generation of singers. It was *A Shropshire Lad* (1896), by A. E. HOUSMAN (1859–   ). Housman's offering was influenced by the ironic detachment of Hardy and the more biting cynicism of Heine. But beneath the pessimistic philosophy there ran a music so appealing in a strain so incongruously buoyant that readers who ordinarily might have been repelled by the thought were fascinated by Housman's tone of voice. After a silence of twenty-six years Housman published a companion volume, significantly entitled *Last Poems* (1922).

Bridging the interval between the Victorian era and the present day, preparing the way for "the younger men," some ten or twelve poets contributed work of more than passing interest. Among these the most notable were GERARD MANLEY HOPKINS (1844–1898), whose extraordinary if dissonant fantasies were not published until 1919; ARTHUR O'SHAUGHNESSY (1844–1881), remembered chiefly because of the ode beginning "We are the music makers"; ROBERT BRIDGES (1844–   ), who became Poet Laureate in 1913, whose work reveals remarkable subtleties of rhythm and mastery of metrics; AUSTIN DOBSON (1840–1912), a past master of *vers de société* and the intricate French forms; ANDREW LANG (1844–   ), a lesser Dobson; JOHN DAVIDSON (1857–1909), whose "Ballad of a Nun" and "A Ballad of Hell" must be numbered among the best of modern ballads; WILLIAM WATSON (1858–   ), a typically Victorian poet whose work gains and suffers by the very rhetoric of the period; STEPHEN PHILLIPS (1868–1915), whose dramas, temporarily successful, did not fulfill the promise of his poetry; and ARTHUR SYMONS (1865–   ), first attracted to the Symbolist movement, and an obvious disciple of Verlaine and Baudelaire: his later work, however, is free from foreign influences and achieves a more restrained sensuousness.

It is still too early to render final judgment on the work of the contemporaries. Insufficient time has elapsed to allow a clear perspective on what, in spite of political disturbances and general disruption, is a period of intellectual fertility. However, it is safe to assume that a few writers have already achieved more than ephemeral notice. Chief among these is JOHN MASEFIELD (1878–). Masefield established himself with *The Everlasting Mercy* (1911) and *The Widow in the Bye Street* (1912), rhymed narratives in the Chaucerian style with a vigor unsurpassed by any poet of his day. Reflecting the very rawness and rigor of life, he emphasized Synge's statement that "the strong things of life are needed in poetry also . . . and it might almost be said that before verse can be human again it must be brutal."

If Masefield represented the extreme of realism, the opposite swing of the pendulum was not without its recorders. WALTER DE LA MARE (1873–), RALPH HODGSON (1871–), and W. H. DAVIES (1870–) created a verse which, though different in particulars, had a common delicacy, an Ariel-like fantasy. Of this unaffiliated trio, Hodgson's poetry was the shyest and most ethereal; de la Mare's the most varied in shifting inflections and the most whimsically macabre; Davies's, piped upon an "oaten straw," the most thoughtlessly birdlike. After Davies, the pastoral note was sounded by JOHN FREEMAN (1881–), MARTIN ARMSTRONG (1882–), and FRANK PREWETT (1893–).

A series of anthologies, first published in 1912, helped to create the group known as the Georgians. There was little similarity of aim or idiom among the various contributors, but a sufficient common interest to form something of a "movement." Its leaders were LASCELLES ABERCROMBIE (1881–), whose *Emblems of Love* vibrated with a nobility of phrase and spirit; RUPERT BROOKE (1887–1915), whose work, strongly influenced by Donne and cut off by his early death, gave promise of ranking with the best of his times; G. K. CHESTERTON

(1874–   ), whose "Lepanto" and other ballads rose above his somewhat too facile paradoxical essays; JOHN DRINKWATER (1882–   ), whose many agreeable lyrics never won the esteem accorded his play, *Abraham Lincoln;* JAMES ELROY FLECKER (1884–1915), another youth whose premature death robbed contemporary poetry of one of its richest talents; WILFRID WILSON GIBSON (1878–   ), an avowed apostle of Masefield; D. H. LAWRENCE (1885–   ), whose darker introspections forced him to abandon the group; HAROLD MONRO (1879–   ), who established a curious intimacy between Man and the inanimate objects he moved among; and JAMES STEPHENS (1882–   ), in whom the Celtic revival found a belated but beautiful echo.

Since the War, a host of young poets have made their bid for fame. Of these one must at least mention SIEGFRIED SASSOON (1886–   ), whose *Counter-Attack* voices the protest of enraged youth against the horrors encountered in the trenches; ROBERT GRAVES (1895–   ), Sassoon's fellow-soldier, whose reactions are expressed in a lighter key and whose more recent work vacillates between "country sentiment" and self-analysis; CHARLOTTE MEW, whom Hardy has hailed as one of the few "great poets" of her day; ANNA WICKHAM (1884–   ), singer of a kind of tortured domesticity; FRANCIS LEDWIDGE (1891–1917), whose twilight-colored verse is dimly reminiscent of Keats; SYLVIA TOWNSEND WARNER, who is equally distinguished in her hard satires and rich intensities; HUMBERT WOLFE (1885–   ), whose *The Unknown Goddess* is full of bittersweet modulations; and the three SITWELLS (EDITH, OSBERT, and SACHEVERELL), by far the most interesting of "the left wing," whose riper work (particularly Edith Sitwell's *Troy Park*) is something more than a successful experiment.

America

Bridging the gap between the New England group and the contemporary poets towers the figure of WALT WHITMAN (1819–1892), who not only was a forerunner of all that is "democratic" in modern literature but has been hailed as a spiritual godfather of the romantic realism which characterizes the present. The first edition of Whitman's *Leaves of Grass* (1855) appeared in the same year as Longfellow's *Hiawatha*, and, though readers of both volumes were then unaware of it, the two books revealed the two poets most definitely American, not so much in their native characteristics but in their essential differences. No greater contrast could be imagined. Longfellow belonged to the century in which he lived; Whitman is not only aligned with the poets writing to-day, but many of his pages, like the later compositions of Beethoven, will yield their complete secret only to the future.

In an era when French forms were coming into their widest popularity and the most skillful technician was hailed as the greatest poet, when delicacy was considered a refinement and healthy strength a vulgarity, when places in Greece or ancient Italy were still considered more worthy of song than Brooklyn Bridge or Manhattan ferry, it is perhaps not to be wondered at that *Leaves of Grass* was received with astonishment, incredulity, and vehement scorn. To-day Whitman is hailed universally as a prophet and pioneer. First recognized in England by Swinburne and Rossetti, he has become a world figure, his elemental and rhapsodic poems having been translated into every language. John Burroughs, his friend and first champion, declared that his work had the power "to open doors and windows, to let down bars rather than to put them up, to dissolve forms, to escape narrow boundaries, to plant the reader on a hill rather than in a corner."

"It was this breadth" (the quotation is from *Modern American Poetry*), "this jubilant acceptance, that made Whitman so keen a lover of casual and ordinary things; he was the first of our poets to reveal 'the glory of the commonplace.' He transmuted, by the intensity of his emotion, material which had been hitherto regarded as too unpoetic for poetry. His long poem 'Song of Myself' is a magnificent example. Here his 'barbaric yawp,' sounded 'over the roofs of the world,' is softened, time and again, to express a lyric ecstasy and naïf wonder. . . .

"It is this large naturalism, this affection for all that is homely and of the soil, that sets Whitman apart from his fellow craftsmen as our first American poet. This blend of familiarity and grandeur, this racy but religious mysticism, animates all his work. It swings with tremendous vigor through 'Crossing Brooklyn Ferry'; it sharpens the sturdy rhythms (and occasional rhymes) of the 'Song of the Broad-Axe'; it beats sonorously through 'Drum-Taps'; it whispers immortally through the 'Memories of President Lincoln' (particularly that magnificent threnody 'When Lilacs Last in the Dooryard Bloom'd' [and the favorite 'O Captain! My Captain!']; it quickens the 'Song of the Open Road' with what Tennyson called 'the glory of going on,' and lifts with a biblical solemnity his Delphic rhapsody, 'Out of the Cradle Endlessly Rocking.'"

Another poet who, only by the accident of chronology, was born in the period of the New England poets, was EMILY DICKINSON (1830–1886). In spirit as well as in the very form of her work, she was altogether in advance of her time. She cared so little for public approval (or even for public appearance) that, although she wrote several hundred poems startling in their originality, she published only three or four during her lifetime—and these were printed almost against her will. She delighted in the use of assonance and half-rhymed vowels, a fondness that at first seems to be only an eccentricity. The surface oddities of her work—the disregard of traditional form, the hit-or-miss grammar, the curious and almost impertinent conceits—limited her readers to an enthusiastic few. Her audience grew only gradually and it was not until almost forty years after her death that she became internationally prominent and her first collected *Complete Poems* made their appearance. Emily Dickinson wrote exclusively of four things—Love, Nature, Life, Death—but she sounded the very depths of these immensities. Her poetry is distinguished not only by its intensity of emotion but by its very brilliance of epithet; her vision was as keen to translate the sharp realities of earth as it was quick to reveal the world recognized only by her spiritual eye.

After Whitman and Emerson, power gave way to pale romanticism and polite banter; there ensued the transition, or what might be called the "post-mortem," period. "Much of our poetry," Thoreau wrote at the time, "has the very best manners but no character." Most of the poets, in an effort to escape a reality they did not wish to face, toyed with artificial fancies and fled to a realm of conscious make-believe. Among the writers who sought relief in superficially oriental themes were BAYARD TAYLOR (1825–1878), RICHARD HENRY STODDARD (1825–1903), and THOMAS BAILEY ALDRICH (1836–1907).

But a new counter-movement was developing, a racy spirit was struggling to express itself. Folk songs were born again when STEPHEN C. FOSTER (1826–1864) composed his "My Old Kentucky Home," "Suwanee River," and "Massa's in De Cold, Cold Ground," and the new

West began to find a voice. Heretofore, all the poetry of "these States" had been produced in the East, but in BRET HARTE (1839–1902) and JOAQUIN MILLER (1841–1913) the West suddenly became articulate. Harte, although born in New York, spent part of his life on the Pacific coast, and it was this period which seems to have made the deepest impression upon him, for most of his many stories and poems deal with California. Though a number of his verses are crudely melodramatic and sentimental, Harte was particularly successful in dialect, his parodies and occasional verses delighting a multitude of readers. Miller, like several other American writers, received scant attention in his native land until he was hailed in England as "a genius from a new world." He was acclaimed "the great interpreter of vigorous America," "the Byron of Oregon," the praise which he received being no more exaggerated than the boisterousness exhibited in his verse. Although most of his grandiose lines seem doomed to extinction, he is still celebrated as the author of "Columbus," one of the most widely quoted of didactic poems.

The South gave birth to her second notable poet in SIDNEY LANIER (1842–1887), whose finer poems are almost as melody-drenched as Swinburne's. He once wrote "whatever turn I have for art is purely musical—poetry being with me a mere tangent into which I shoot," and this overemphasis on euphony proved to be Lanier's greatest weakness, the poet being at his best in a few ballads and the spontaneous "Marshes of Glynn."

Dialect poetry of a particularly ingratiating type found its chief exponents in JAMES WHITCOMB RILEY (1849–1916), EUGENE FIELD (1850–1895), and PAUL LAURENCE DUNBAR (1872–1906), Dunbar's negro interpretations being a model for the rest of his race.

Another reaction set in at the beginning of the Eighteen-Nineties. Differing in every way from the *fin de siècle* revolt of this decade in England, the insurgence demanded a more athletic energy, a demand that was answered by the three volumes of *Songs from Vagabondia* (1894, 1896, 1900), the result of collaboration between RICHARD HOVEY (1864–1900) and BLISS CARMAN (1861–   ). Hovey's spirit was the more exuberant and went deeper into experience, his being an unusual combination of high spirits and high seriousness. Following these gay apostles of outdoor vigor, the "interim" poets challenged attention. WILLIAM VAUGHN MOODY (1869–1910) raised a protesting voice against the cheapening of patriotism and EDWIN MARKHAM (1852–   ) aroused the country with his ringing if rhetorical "The Man with the Hoe."

The following so-called "new era" in American poetry may be said to date from 1914, in which year various tendencies crystallized into movements, and many of the poets who later were to challenge attention issued their first volumes. As in the case of contemporary English poetry, it is impossible to form conclusive estimates of the work of living writers, not only because there is insufficient perspective, but because the work of these poets is not yet completed. Time, the coldest and most cruel of anthologists, will render the final judgment. Meanwhile, there are a few writers for whom one may predict some sort of permanence and a host of others whose contributions deserve at least passing notice. Among the first of these is EDWIN ARLINGTON ROBINSON (1869–   ). His first volume, *Children of the Night*, issued as early as 1897, used a concisely epigrammatic speech in sharp contrast to the rhetoric of his predecessors, and his *Collected Poems* (1921) reveals a dry and astringent idiom which, though ranging the world for its themes, is New

England in its very clipped precision. His extensive work is full of brilliant condensations and a sympathy with all phases of humanity, particularly with those lost dreamers whom the world appraises as mediocrities and failures.

On an equally high level with Robinson, ROBERT FROST (1875–   ), in his trilogy of New England (*North of Boston, Mountain Interval,* and *New Hampshire*) discloses a poetry which, while local to the very core, goes far deeper than surface idiosyncrasies. Never has poetry been written closer to the earth, and never has any writer communicated a greater love of it. But Frost is more concerned with the soul than with the soil; a true pastoral poet, he has written lyrics and "grace-notes" as well as philosophic monologues which may take their place with the spiritual bucolics of Vergil and Wordsworth.

In direct opposition to the reticence of Frost and Robinson, one encounters the abrupt declamations of CARL SANDBURG (1878–   ). Because he drew most of his material from the Middle West and, for a while, concerned himself with steel mills and slaughterhouses, city streets and farm laborers, Sandburg was called "the laureate of industrial America." But though his irregular rhythms sounded the immense energies of modern machinery, and though he employed slang with a pioneering gusto, Sandburg was brutal only when brutality was his theme. If his *Chicago Poems* (1916), *Cornhuskers,* and *Smoke and Steel* contain some of the most raucous ejaculations, they also whisper some of the tenderest phrases in modern poetry.

Two other poets of the Mid-West established themselves at the same time: EDGAR LEE MASTERS (1869–   ), and VACHEL LINDSAY (1879–   ). Masters's *Spoon River Anthology* (1915) was not only a document but a landmark; a sequence of revealing epitaphs. This collection far surpassed the author's many subsequent volumes, although *Domesday Book* (1920) is an ambitious effort to act as an American counterpart to Browning's *The Ring and the Book*. Vachel Lindsay's *General Booth Enters into Heaven* (1913) was the first to use the insistent rhythm and tympanic rhymes which the author later exploited in *The Congo and Other Poems* and the following volumes recently issued in *Collected Poems* (1925). In his chants, Lindsay captures the spiritual as well as the aural syncopation of the United States. He accomplishes a curious wedding of ragtime and religion; he brings jazz into poetry but remains as much the missionary as the minstrel. JAMES OPPENHEIM (1882–   ) is a rhapsodist of a different order. His sources are definitely the minor Hebrew prophets, and *The Sea*, a collection of his preceding volumes, is a blend of biblical sonority and Whitmanic prophecy.

Certain premature appraisers have attempted to sum up the period as "an era of uncertain experiments," and, though the decade beginning with 1914 was as distinguished in performance as in promise, it must be admitted that at no time in the history of American literature have there been so many different innovators. Of these, AMY LOWELL (1874–1925) is likely to be remembered longest. As propagandist she was the leader of the Imagists, the group which stressed a *visual* poetry and "the use of the *exact* word, not the merely decorative word"; as critic, she published the highly controversial and always stimulating *Tendencies in Modern American Poetry;* as poet, her volumes (of which *Pictures of the Floating World* [1919] is typical) disclosed a command of the lacquered phrase, an ability to capture the minute disturbances of light and motion, an uncanny power of impelling, curbing, and quickening a movement. "H. D." and JOHN GOULD FLETCHER (1886–   ), were two of the most prominent Imagists, "H. D.'s" *Collected Poems* (1925) being a monument or rather a delicately carved frieze which seems likely to outlive the very name of the group.

Contemporary verse shows the impress and at times the influence of half a dozen other experimenters. The most important of these are: EZRA POUND (1885–   ), whose early poems have a strange beauty and whose later work is sunk in theory; T. S. ELIOT (1888–   ), whose *The Waste Land* (1922) is a minor epic of disintegration and nostalgia and whose "The Love Song of J. Alfred Prufrock" is a brilliant study of disillusion; ALFRED KREYMBORG (1883–   ), who delights in a puppetlike whimsicality; MAXWELL BODENHEIM (1892–   ), whose acrobatic ironies descend obliquely from Euphues; MARIANNE MOORE, whose lines, vacillating in the borderland between poetry and prose, are packed with witty criticism; WALLACE STEVENS, whose *Harmonium* (1923) maintains a detached elegance; JOHN CROWE RANSOM (1888–   ), whose piquant accents distinguish *Chills and Fever* (1924); and E. E. CUMMINGS, whose *Tulips and Chimneys* (1924) is a bizarre combination of typographical absurdity and lyric suavity.

If "the new poetry" is distinguished for nothing else, it assumes importance because of its lyricists. The work of the women alone establishes this; never before has there been such a singing sorority. LIZETTE WOODWORTH REESE (1856–   ) was the forerunner of the younger women who delight in an unsentimental directness, sparse imagery, and immediacy of communication. The two most deservedly popular of these younger voices are EDNA ST. VINCENT MILLAY (1892–   ) and SARA TEASDALE (1883–   ). Miss Millay rose suddenly into fame with her amazing "Renascence" (the title-poem of her first volume, published in 1917), which she wrote at the age of nineteen. The subsequent *Second April* (1921) secured her high position. Sara Teasdale's *Flame and Shadow* (1921) and the later, more somber lyrics have the quality of folk songs and recall, in their poignance, the spirit of Christina Rossetti. Other women whose lyrics deserve more notice than can be given them in this limited space are ELINOR WYLIE, LOUISE BOGAN, ANNA HEMPSTEAD BRANCH, LÉONIE ADAMS, HAZEL HALL, VIRGINIA MOORE, LOLA RIDGE, GENEVIEVE TAGGARD, and JEAN STARR UNTERMEYER.

Although the men have developed a more acrid lyricism, special praise must be given to the subtle and plangent music of CONRAD AIKEN (1889–), especially in *Punch: The Immortal Liar* and *Priapus and the Pool;* JOHN HALL WHEELOCK (1886–), whose early and somewhat Henleyesque *The Human Fantasy* was succeeded by the graver *The Black Panther;* WILLIAM ROSE BENET (1886–), and STEPHEN VINCENT BENÉT (1898–), brothers in blood and balladry; WITTER BYNNER (1881–), ARTHUR DAVISON FICKE (1883–), LOUIS UNTERMEYER (1885–), ORRICK JOHNS (1887–), JOSEPH AUSLANDER (1897–), ROBINSON JEFFERS, and COUNTÉE CULLEN (1903–).

Although a great quantity of militant poetry was produced in America during the War, practically nothing remains. The names of only two war-poets have survived, and each of these is remembered because of a single poem: "Trees" (which is in no sense a war-poem) by JOYCE KILMER (1886–1918) and "I Have a Rendezvous with Death" by ALAN SEEGER (1888–1916).

The most "modern" appraiser of contemporary poetry must also take into account the considerable body of work definitely in the tradition of formal "poetic speech." He should not neglect to mention the more conservative work of GEORGE SANTAYANA (1863–), WILLIAM ELLERY LEONARD (1876–), GEORGE STERLING (1869–), and JOHN G. NEIHARDT (1881–), whose chief work is an epic series celebrating the winning of the West. In short, every type of verse, from the most classical to the most wildly experimental, has been and is still being sounded by the living poets.

A SUMMARIZED BIBLIOGRAPHY

The following volumes are classified according to their kind, and though the lists are necessarily limited, most of the important volumes of the periods are tabulated. An asterisk (*) in front of a title means that the book thus marked is either of a technical nature or is recommended for advanced students.

General

For a general consideration of poetry, the following titles will repay study:

AN INTRODUCTION TO POETRY. *Hubbell and Beatty.* The Macmillan Company, 1922.

* THE ESSENTIALS OF POETRY. *William Allan Neilson.* Houghton Mifflin Company, 1912.

ENJOYMENT OF POETRY. *Max Eastman.* Charles Scribner's Sons, 1915.

AMERICAN LITERATURE. *Percy H. Boynton.* Ginn and Company, 1923.

* CONVENTION AND REVOLT IN POETRY. *John Livingston Lowes.* Houghton Mifflin Company, 1919.

THE KINDS OF POETRY. *John Erskine.* Duffield and Company, 1923.

AMERICAN LITERATURE. *Charles F. Richardson.* G. P. Putnam's Sons, 1889.

A DEFENSE OF POETRY. *Percy Bysshe Shelley.*

* A NEW DEFENSE OF POETRY (in *Heart of Man and Other Papers*). *George E. Woodberry.* Harcourt, Brace and Company.

* THE FORMS OF ENGLISH POETRY. *C. F. Johnson.*

* SCEPTICISMS: NOTES ON CONTEMPORARY POETRY. *Conrad Aiken.* Alfred A. Knopf, 1919.

* ON ENGLISH POETRY ("being an irregular approach to the psychology of the art, from evidence mainly subjective"). *Robert Graves.* Alfred A. Knopf, 1922.

STUDIES OF CONTEMPORARY POETRY. (Confined to a study of the contemporary English poets.) *Mary C. Sturgeon.* Dodd, Mead and Company, 1919.

* SOME CONTEMPORARY POETS. (This is also confined to recent English poets.) *Harold Monro.* Leonard Parsons (London), 1920.

* A NEW STUDY OF ENGLISH POETRY. (Twelve essays on such subjects as "Poetry and Rhythm," "Poetry and Education," and "British Ballads.") *Henry Newbolt.* E. P. Dutton and Company, 1919.

* The Theory of Poetry. *Lascelles Abercrombie.* Harcourt, Brace and
    Company, 1926.
* New Voices. *Marguerite Wilkinson.* The Macmillan Company, 1921.
* American Poetry Since 1900. *Louis Untermeyer.* Henry Holt
    and Company, 1923.

Collections

It would be impossible to list the many anthologies which
cover the ground with varying thoroughness. However, as
reference volumes and for those who wish to study the poets in
greater detail, the following larger collections may be recommended.

The Golden Treasury of Songs and Poems. Selected and arranged
    by *Francis T. Palgrave.* Thomas Y. Crowell & Company, 1883.
    (330 pages.)
The Home Book of Verse. Edited by *Burton E. Stevenson.* Henry
    Holt and Company, 1918. (4000 pages.)
The Oxford Book of English Verse. Edited by *A. T. Quiller-Couch.*
    Oxford University Press, 1919. (1080 pages.)
* The Oxford Book of Victorian Verse. Edited by *A. T. Quiller-
    Couch.* Oxford University Press, 1919. (1000 pages.)
An American Anthology. (From 1787 to 1900.) Edited by *Edmund
    Clarence Stedman.* Houghton Mifflin Company, 1900. (860 pages.)
A Victorian Anthology. (From 1837 to 1895.) Edited by *Edmund
    Clarence Stedman.* Houghton Mifflin Company, 1895. (740 pages.)
Romantic and Victorian Poetry. Edited by *C. E. Andrews* and *M.
    O. Percival.* A. A. Adams & Company (Columbus, Ohio), 1924.
    (980 pages.)
* The New Poetry: An Anthology of Twentieth-Century Verse
    in English. Edited by *Harriet Monroe* and *Alice Corbin Henderson.*
    The Macmillan Company, 1923. (611 pages.)
An Anthology of Modern Verse. (Devoted exclusively to recent
    English poets.) Chosen by *A. Methuen.* Methuen and Company
    (London), 1921. (240 pages.)
Modern British Poetry. (From 1840 to 1925.) Revised and En-
    larged Edition. Edited by *Louis Untermeyer.* Harcourt, Brace and
    Company, 1925. (388 pages.)
Modern American Poetry. (From 1830 to 1925.) Revised and
    Enlarged Edition. Edited by *Louis Untermeyer.* Harcourt, Brace
    and Company, 1925. (621 pages.)

Collections for Younger Readers

The Home Book of Verse for Young Folks. Edited by *Burton E.
    Stevenson.* Henry Holt and Company, 1915.
Golden Numbers. Chosen and Classified by *Kate Douglas Wiggin* and
    Nora Archibald Smith. McClure, Phillips & Co., 1903.

THE LISTENING CHILD. Selected by *Lucy W. Thacher*. The Macmillan Company, Revised Edition, 1924.

RAINBOW GOLD. Edited by *Sara Teasdale*. The Macmillan Company, 1922.

POEMS FOR YOUTH. Edited by *William Rose Benét*. E. P. Dutton and Co., 1925.

COME HITHER. Edited by *Walter de la Mare*. Alfred A. Knopf, 1923.

OPEN GATES. Edited by *Susan Thompson Spaulding* and *Francis Trow Spaulding*. Houghton Mifflin Company, 1924.

THIS SINGING WORLD. Edited by *Louis Untermeyer*. Harcourt, Brace and Company, 1923. (Junior Edition, 1926.)

YESTERDAY AND TODAY: A COMPARATIVE ANTHOLOGY OF POETRY. Edited with notes by *Louis Untermeyer*. Harcourt, Brace and Company, 1926.

Ballads

The best collections of older or popular ballads are, without doubt, the following:

PERCY'S RELIQUES OR RELIQUES OF ANCIENT ENGLISH POETRY. *Thomas Percy, Lord Bishop of Dromore*. Thomas Y. Crowell and Company.

THE BALLAD BOOK. Edited by *William Allingham*.

THE OXFORD BOOK OF BALLADS. Edited by *A. T. Quiller-Couch*. Oxford University Press.

* BALLADS AND LYRICS OF LOVE. Edited by *Frank Sidgwick*. F. A. Stokes Company.

* LEGENDARY BALLADS. Edited by *Frank Sidgwick*. F. A. Stokes Company.

ENGLISH AND SCOTTISH POPULAR BALLADS. Edited from the collection of Francis J. Child by *Helen Child Sargent* and *George Lyman Kittredge*. Houghton Mifflin Company, 1904.

A particularly splendid résumé is Andrew Lang's article on the ballad in *The Encyclopædia Britannica*.

Excellent examples of the modern American ballad may be found in:

COWBOY SONGS AND OTHER FRONTIER BALLADS. Collected and edited by *John A. Lomax*. The Macmillan Company.

* POETIC ORIGINS AND THE BALLAD. *Professor Louise Pound*. The Macmillan Company, 1921.

AMERICAN BALLADS AND SONGS. Collected by *Professor Louise Pound*. Charles Scribner's Sons, 1922.

THE BOOK OF AMERICAN NEGRO POETRY. Edited by *James Weldon Johnson*. Harcourt, Brace and Company.

KENTUCKY MOUNTAIN SONGS AND LONESOME TUNES. (With music.) *Loraine Wyman* and *Howard Brockway*. Ditson and Company.

The French Forms

The two best collections as well as the two best analyses of the French forms are:

* BALLADES AND RONDEAUS, SESTINAS, VILLANELLES, etc. Selected by *Gleeson White*. The Walter Scott Publishing Company.
LYRIC FORMS FROM FRANCE: THEIR HISTORY AND THEIR USE. Edited by *Helen Louise Cohen*. Harcourt, Brace and Company.

Vers de Société

(Occasional Verse)

The collections of *vers de société* are almost as numerous as the usual type of anthology. Carolyn Wells has been a pioneer in this field; three of her most enticing collections are listed below.

A VERS DE SOCIÉTÉ ANTHOLOGY. Collected by *Carolyn Wells*. Charles Scribner's Sons.
A WHIMSEY ANTHOLOGY. Collected by *Carolyn Wells*. Charles Scribner's Sons.
A PARODY ANTHOLOGY. Collected by Carolyn Wells. Charles Scribner's Sons.

Other standard volumes are:

AMERICAN FAMILIAR VERSE. Edited by *Brander Matthews*. Longmans, Green and Company.
VERS DE SOCIÉTÉ. Edited by *Charles H. Jones*. Henry Holt and Company.
LYRA ELEGANTIARUM. Edited by *Frederick Locker-Lampson*. Ward, Lock and Company (London).
THE LITTLE BOOK OF SOCIETY VERSE. Compiled by *Claude Moore Fuess* and *Harold Crawford Stearns*. Houghton Mifflin Company.
A LITTLE BOOK OF LIGHT VERSE. Edited by *Anthony C. Deane*. Dodd, Mead and Company.
A TREASURY OF HUMOROUS POETRY. Edited by *Frederick Lawrence Knowles*. Dana Estes and Company.

Free Verse

The best discussion of free verse occurs in two volumes, both of them rather technical, which present two almost opposed points of view. These two volumes are:

* TENDENCIES IN MODERN AMERICAN POETRY. *Amy Lowell*. The Macmillan Company.
* THE RHYTHM OF PROSE. *William Morrison Patterson*. Columbia University Press.

(Amy Lowell's introduction to her *Can Grande's Castle* contains not only the basic idea of free verse, but also a complete explanation of "polyphonic prose.")

The Epic

The best consideration of the epic principle is to be found in:

ENGLISH EPIC AND HEROIC POETRY. *Professor W. MacNeile Dixon, M. A.* J. M. Dent and Sons (London), 1911.

The Sonnet

The most thorough consideration as well as the best historical survey of the subject of the sonnet itself is:

THE ENGLISH SONNET. T. W. H. CROSSLAND. Dodd, Mead and Company, 1917.

There are three general compilations which are excellent in themselves and especially interesting as comparative collections; the first covers the field from Henry Howard, Earl of Surrey (1517–1547), to the New England poets; the second is devoted entirely to the poets of the Nineteenth Century.

THE BOOK OF THE SONNET. (Two volumes.) Edited by *Leigh Hunt* and *S. Adams Lee.* Roberts Brothers.
SONNETS OF THIS CENTURY. (With a critical introduction on the sonnet.) *William Sharp.*
THE GOLDEN BOOK OF ENGLISH SONNETS. Selected by *William Robertson.* Harrap & Company (London), 1913.

The Lyric

The best discussion as well as the most comprehensive analyses of the English lyric are to be found in:

* LYRIC POETRY. (From the earliest Norman melodies to the literary lyrics of the late Victorians.) *Ernest Rhys.* E. P. Dutton and Company, 1913.

There are several collections of purely lyrical verses, the best being:

ENGLISH LYRICAL POETRY (1500–1700). Edited by *Frederic Ives Carpenter.* Charles Scribner's Sons.
SELECTIONS FROM MODERN POETS. Made by *J. C. Squire.* Martin Secker (London), 1921.
SHORTER LYRICS OF THE TWENTIETH CENTURY, 1900–1922. Selected by *W. H. Davies.* The Poetry Bookshop (London).

INDEX OF AUTHORS QUOTED